Confessions of a Financial Planner
Secrets to a Secure Retirement

David D. Holland
CERTIFIED FINANCIAL PLANNER™
Certified Public Accountant
Personal Financial Specialist
Chartered Financial Consultant®

Published 2011
Printed in the United States of America

ISBN 978-0-615-46629-3

www.confessionsofafinancialplanner.com

This Book Is Whole-Heartedly Dedicated

To My Wife, Toni,
Whose Beauty and Intellect Are Only Surpassed by Her Patience,

To My Three Children, Zachary, Mary, and Grace,
Who Challenge Me to Be Better Than I Am Every Day,

To My Loving and Selfless Parents, Cary and Connie Holland,
Who Tirelessly Built My Moral Compass,

To My Entire Family,
Who Are Quick to Overlook My Shortcomings,
Yet Trumpet My Accomplishments,

And to My Dedicated Team at Holland Financial,
Who, Every Day, *Help Retirees of Today, and Tomorrow,*
Achieve Their Financial Dreams.

Acknowledgements

Praise God, from Whom All Blessings Flow;
Praise Him, All Creatures Here Below;
Praise Him Above, Ye Heavenly Host;
Praise Father, Son, and Holy Ghost.

Let me now also thank a few mortals for their contributions to this book:

The Editors – Toni Holland (the patient, smart, and beautiful wife who also has a Masters Degree in Literature) who made sure the final version of this book is readable, Kalon M. Hoard (my Chief Compliance Officer and Senior Vice President at Holland Advisory Services, Inc.) who made sure it is both fair and accurate, and Christina Kohl-Merklin (run-on-sentence wrangler, photographer, image enhancer, and Creative Director for Holland Productions, Inc.) who superbly managed the content.

The Contributors – Andrew Thrasher, Hady LaGrotta, Jeff Thrasher, Angel Pinkerton, and Shannon McAvoy did research and expressed opinions about what should be included in this book.

The Illustrator – the very talented John Hambrook who turned my crude sketches into black-and-white masterpieces. If you like what you see and need his help, call John at In-House Communications: 262-657-3777.

The Encouragers – Michael H. Mastowski (the wise business partner) and Arlene "Pat" Detweiler (my very dedicated assistant and personal confidant) kept me writing when I wanted to stop.

The Supporters – I thank the three hundred clients who made this book financially possible. *You* already know a lot of what's in this book.

The Mentors – besides my family, five men encouraged the spark they saw in me: Ray Mercer, John E. McEldowney, Cory T. Walker, J. Hyatt Brown, and Richard M. Pankratz.

The English Teachers – four special women guided, molded, and taught me because they *could* and *would*: Marion Monaghan (12th grade), Heidi Graham (10th and 11th grade), Wilma Graham (8th and 9th grade), and my grandmother, Hazel Holland (every morning before elementary school).

Table of Contents

Foreword
Preface

The Threats to a Secure Retirement and the Need for Planning

Secret #1: The Need for Planning
Secret #2: How to Eliminate the Threats to Your Retirement
Secret #3: Don't Let Emotions Ruin Your Retirement
Secret #4: Live Long and Prosper (by Planning Well)
Secret #5: *Dollar-Cost-Ravaging* Only Works in the Movies
Secret #6: Gold, Guns, Chickens, and Inflation

The Planning Needed to Overcome the Threats

Secret #7: Do You Have Good Investments?
Secret #8: How to Build a Retirement Income Plan

Investments as Part of Your Retirement Plan

Secret #9: Commonly Used Investment Strategies
Secret #10: Overview of Investment Securities
Secret #11: "The Skinny" on Fixed-Income Securities
Secret #12: Mutual Funds as Part of Your Retirement Plan
Secret #13: Investment and Financial Product Fees

Banking and Insurance as Part of Your Retirement Plan

Secret #14: Should You Bank on Your Bank?
Secret #15: Insurance Companies: Big Buildings, Lots of Money
Secret #16: The Proper Use of Life Insurance
Secret #17: Long-term Care Insurance
Secret #18: Annuities as Part of Your Retirement Plan

Conclusion

Foreword

I met David Holland in 2003 while I was working as an annuity marketing representative. My position as a "sales coach" with a marketing company required me to present products to insurance agents and financial planners across the country. My task was to assure them that my products were the best "safe-money" vehicles in the marketplace. I truly believed that they were, so I made my "pitch" with the utmost confidence.

When David was randomly assigned to me, I began to work strategically to convince him that he should recommend my products to his clients. I say "strategically" because David questioned and challenged me in new ways about the products I showed him. As David fired questions at me I began to think, "Wow, this guy is an enigma." I had never run across such a detail-oriented adviser who truly cared about what he did for his clients. There was no doubt in my mind that David would be a world-class adviser …and when that happened, I wanted to make sure that he would use my products for the financial plans he built for his clients.

There came a point when I realized that David had some questions that even *I* couldn't answer. I contacted the insurance company that I represented and requested that the Head Actuary speak to David. This was the one person who could help him understand exactly how particular financial products were built and how they worked. I was told that *no one had ever made this request*; however, I also knew that I had never dealt with an adviser like this before. David, in my opinion, needed a direct conversation with the designer of the product before he would recommend it to a single client. A conference call was scheduled and a lengthy conversation was held. This phone call was pivotal. David gained total confidence in my products. Within a few years, David had become not only my largest producing adviser, but one of the top advisers in the country.

David Holland has a genuine passion for protecting and advising his clients. He has baffled some salespeople with his "do what is best for the client" and "if it ain't broke, don't fix it" approach to helping people. He is committed to ushering baby boomers, retirees, and seniors into their "golden years" with financial security. I believe that David's success stems from living life with integrity and keeping his clients' best interests at heart.

Today, David is my "semi" silent business partner. I'm the president of Retiree Adviser Marketing, Inc., an insurance marketing organization that David and I started back in 2007. Our company helps advisers from all over the country find the best insurance products for their clients. David and I talk almost daily about the ever-changing financial industry and the new ways we can help advisers do the best job for their clients. David was a big feather in my cap when he became my top adviser and I count myself fortunate to have him as my partner…but, most all, I am proud to call him my friend.

We all have a natural desire to chase and fulfill our dreams in life. I know this book will provide you with a new and helpful direction, and it will enlighten you so that you will take the right steps towards personal financial security.

- Mike Mastowski

Preface

We live during uncertain financial, economic, and political times. While many threats and obstacles may stand between you and a secure retirement, you can have a greater chance of achieving your financial dreams <u>if you plan</u>. Reading this book is a good step in that direction.

When was the last time you heard of someone working for <u>one</u> company his or her whole life? Aside from teachers, government employees, and military personnel, it is unusual to find someone who has given twenty or more years to one employer.

American employment has changed significantly over the last thirty years. Businesses have evolved to become much more flexible and efficient in order to compete in our global economy. Predictable, long-term employment has become rare. Companies just don't give out gold watches as incentives anymore and most people don't work long enough for a company to receive one *even if they did.*

In the past, long-term, one employer careers have had their advantages. It used to be that employees:

- Felt more secure in their employment
- Received robust pensions (with survivorship benefits)
- Received health insurance (with no employee contribution)

According to a recent U.S. Bureau of Labor Statistics report (www.bls.gov, September 23, 2010), today's workers change jobs about every four years. Many of today's retirees (and those approaching retirement) have worked for several employers. Furthermore, those healthy pensions of yesterday are not as common today. Getting your retirement "right" has become a lot more complicated than simply multiplying the number of years you worked by the average salary earned for the last five years of your employment.

After nearly twenty years of financial services experience, I am convinced that retirement planning doesn't have to be hard, complicated, or stressful. And that is why I wrote this book.

Today's retiree faces many uncertainties, challenges, and questions. While some retirees still get a pension, a majority of today's retirees arrive at their golden years with Social Security, a 401k, personal investments, and a house. In other words, the typical retiree has a lump sum of money and must decide how to invest it to meet their post-employment needs.

To improve your chances of a secure retirement, we need to cover four key areas in this book:

- ✓ How to eliminate the threats to your retirement security
- ✓ How to make sure you have good investments
- ✓ How to build a personalized retirement income plan
- ✓ How to incorporate investments and insurance into your plan

By the time you've reached the back cover of this book, I am confident that you will have a better understanding of how you can achieve a successful retirement.

I also hope this book brings you several steps closer to peace of mind about your financial future. I wish you a joy-filled and secure retirement!

– David D. Holland

Section I

The Threats to a Secure Retirement and the Need for Planning

Secret #1: The Need for Planning

I certainly don't envy today's retirees. As we plod our way into the new millennium, there are plenty of reasons for Americans to be concerned about their financial futures and their retirements:

New Millennium Challenges and Uncertainties

- Expanding role of government
- Polarization of American political system
- Continued war against terrorists and their supporters
- Continued role of America as the *world's policeman*
- Increasing longevity (retirement assets need to last longer)
- Unemployment and underemployment
- Continued bank failures
- Sluggish housing and auto sales
- Surging number of Social Security recipients
- Governmental refusal to enforce <u>existing</u> immigration laws
- Swelling national debt
- Increasing federal income taxation
- Financial scams that steal the trust and finances of many Americans
- Regulatory oversight that has failed to protect our overall financial system (as well as individual investors)
- Financial markets that fluctuate over news from around the world (sometimes for no good reason at all)
- 24/7 media coverage that makes sure that every person on the face of the earth knows about all *bad* news

If you are about to retire or are already retired, these difficulties should be of special concern to you. Let's face it: how much time do you have to get your financial house in order? How much time do you have to recover from these challenges and from the mistakes you make on your own?

Despite the obvious need for planning for life's uncertainties and challenges, studies have shown that many Americans spend more time *planning their next vacation* than they do on planning their retirement.

Once Upon a Time . . . It Sure Seemed Easier

When times are good, planning ahead can seem unnecessary, and there have been times when American retirees *have gotten away with it.* To give us some perspective of where we are today, here's a graph of what the stock market did during the last fifty years (usually, financial folks use the S&P 500 index as a representation for the overall market, so that's what I've done here with data from Standard & Poor's). Below are the cumulative returns for the market for each ten-year period since 1960.

Cumulative 10-Year Returns

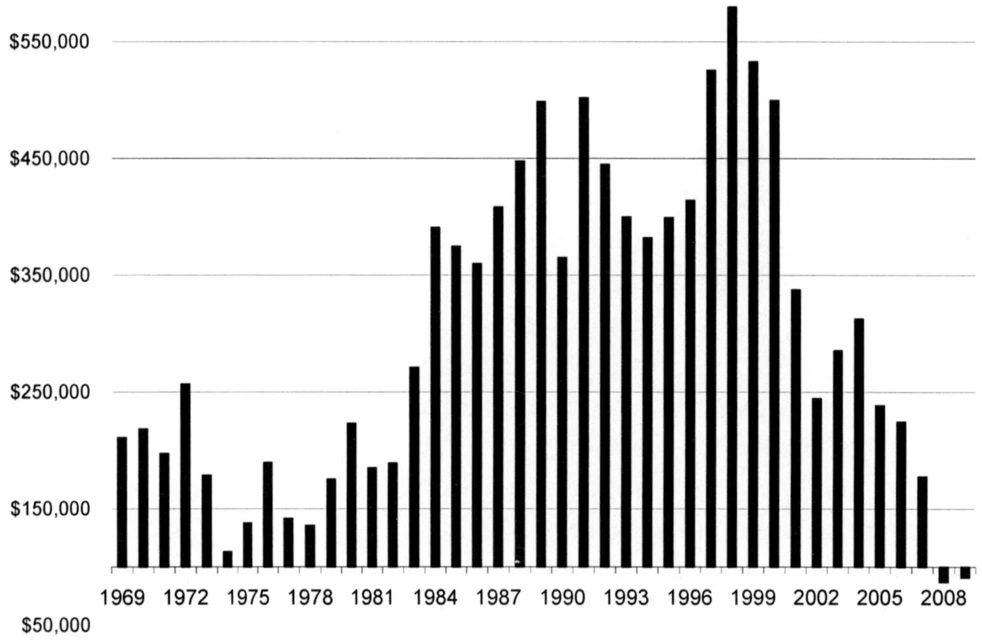

For example, the stock market grew 111% during the first ten-year period shown in this graph (which ended in 1969). So, if you had invested $100,000 on the first day of 1960, it would have grown to $211,005 by the end of 1969. The average annual compound return for that ten-year period was 7.75%. Now, let's look at the ten-year period that ended in 2009. Drum roll, please . . . wow, you would have lost a total of 9.1%! That same $100,000 invested in 2000 would have dropped to $90,900. That's an average loss of 1% each year for that ten-year span..

The Dead Decade

Yes, I know I have ignored taxes, investment fees, and inflation in this simple comparison. I also know that no one can invest directly in a stock market index. The point is that retirees of yesteryear got a lot more help from the stock market than retirees of today. Retirees of today face a very different reality, and the need for retirement planning has never been greater.

For a cold dose of this investing reality, just take a look at this year-by-year review of the stock market for 2000 through 2009. The solid line on the graph shows the stock market's wild and disappointing ride for the ten years ending in 2009. Not good, especially when you compare that performance to a hypothetical investment earning just 2% each year during the same period.

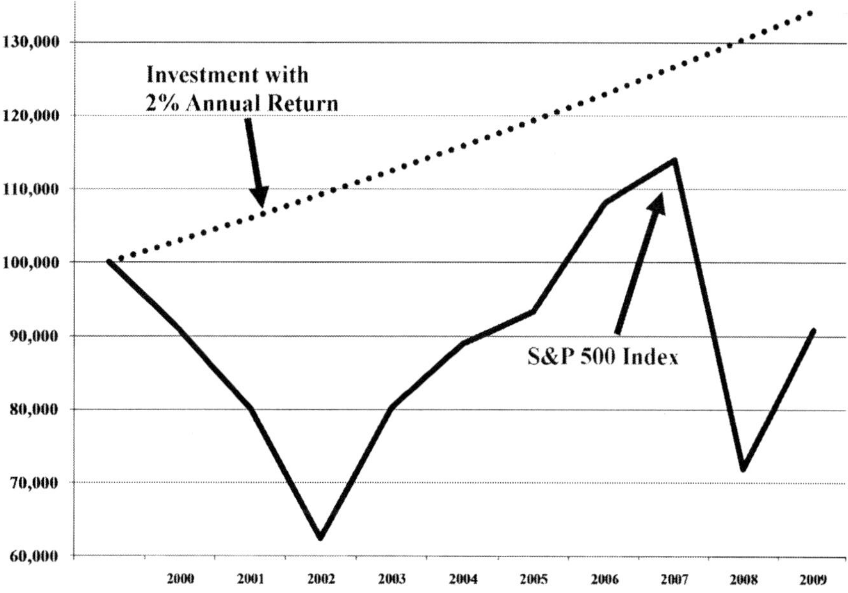

With this kind of poor stock market performance, you don't need to be a CERTIFIED FINANCIAL PLANNER™ practitioner to know how difficult it would be to accumulate funds to draw on later. To maintain their retirement income, many retirees suddenly found themselves unprepared and in the difficult position of having to liquidate their investment principal during this volatile period of time. The results were not pretty. And for some, irreparable damage was done.

Get With the Program! Build *Your* Plan for Retirement Security.

Planning for a secure retirement means facing up to this new investing reality of disappointing, and potentially devastating, market performance. We need to make sure our own retirement plan (if we have one) is built to withstand market downturns for a sustained period. I have helped retirees deal with many challenges and uncertainties. I have also seen people make wise choices with their finances and experience true peace of mind when they take the time to map out their future and deploy their retirement assets properly (that's the point of a financial plan).

When uncertainties arise (ironically, as they *always* do), we get a strong urge to do something about them. We wish we had planned better. The failure to plan ahead has caused otherwise reasonable people to panic and to make bad decisions about their money and their retirement. Some of these mistakes have ended in bankruptcy and utter despair.

"Today" always seems more uncertain than yesterday because our feelings are magnified by our current awareness. Typically, time and distance from uncertain and uncomfortable events tend to tame the experience until our recollection becomes, "it wasn't all that bad." Consider how you feel today about September 11th versus how you felt on that terrible day. Most people can quickly recall where they were and what they thought and felt. Is your emotional response to those events as strong *now* as it was on 9/11? Probably not, but that doesn't make you insensitive or un-American. It is just the way our minds work.

I've talked with retirees who worry about their retirement, yet remarkably, some still won't take the time to build a financial plan to deal with obstacles that can get in the way of their retirement goals. Often, people procrastinate and simply put off planning for their futures. The financial carnage of the 2000s should be more than enough reason to start planning.

Don't let your concerns about your financial future fade with time. Build a financial plan today to protect and secure your retirement tomorrow.

Do You Want Fries with That?

What outcome do you need or want? What do your retirement assets need to do? Based on your individual situation, your retirement nest egg might need to provide for a variety of specific needs. No one has unlimited resources, so we need to plan *realistically* with what we've got. It is not unusual for our desired outcomes to exceed what our retirement assets can provide. So what do we do first? I typically recommend that we start with what you actually need.

For example, let's say that you needed $3,000 in monthly income to cover expenses before you retired. If we paid off the remaining mortgage balance, we'd get to subtract the monthly payment of $1,000. If we plan to spend an average of $500 on travel, we'd add that back in. In this basic example, we would want $2,500 per month in lifetime retirement income. If the nest egg isn't big enough to do this, then adjustments might be required. Of course, monthly income is just one of several needs to be met.

Current Monthly Income Budget:	$3,000
Mortgage Payment Eliminated:	- 1,000
Travel Budget	+ 500
New Monthly Income Budget	$2,500

Secret #2: How to Eliminate the Threats to Your Retirement

After a lifetime of hard work and personal sacrifice, most retirees look forward to relaxation and a variety of pleasant activities during their "golden years." This lifestyle shift, however, is not the time to lower your guard because serious threats remain that can damage your retirement. I'm not talking about a home invasion or losing your wallet. I'm talking about real financial events that can drain your retirement resources. If they are not adequately addressed with solid retirement planning and the right investment and financial products, these "threat needles" could seriously *puncture* your retirement lifestyle.

We should also acknowledge that there are some financial threats over which we have little control. Unfortunately, it is these very same threats that get sensationalized, exaggerated coverage by the 24/7, ratings-driven media. Lethargic economic policies, mushrooming national debt, looming tax increases, and the expanding role of government can only be dealt with in one way: at the voting booth. Now let's move on to the threats that, with some smart planning, we can manage or eliminate completely.

Cash is King

<u>Threat #1 - Cash Emergencies</u>: There's a reason they say that "cash is king." When you need it, you need it! It doesn't matter why.

So where's the threat? The threat lies in the reality of "when you need it, you need it." If an emergency occurs and you need cash to deal with a problem, then you are going to find a way to get the cash right away. Without an adequate cash reserve, your next step will probably be to borrow funds or liquidate investments; that's the threat. If you are forced to borrow funds quickly, you might have to pay a higher interest rate or agree to other unfavorable terms. If you have investments that can be liquidated, the threat is having to sell those investments at a bad time. If your investments have suffered a loss due to a market drop, and that is the time when you need some emergency cash, bad news! Now you've got to sell investment holdings that are down in value, and you might only get 70 or 80 cents on the dollar. The unfortunate result is that you've got to liquidate more stocks or mutual funds to get the same cash.

What's the fix? Build up a cash reserve. Many experts say you need a cash reserve equal to three to six months of living expenses. This is not a bad rule of thumb, but can we give it a little more thought? What can go wrong in your personal situation that can cause you to need a lot of cash? Add up all of your insurance deductibles. If everything breaks at the same time, how much would that cost you? What if your roof needs to be repaired? Is your car still under warranty? Add up all of these potential outlays and then assume that they were to happen simultaneously!

Health Insurance Deductible
Car Insurance Deductible
Homeowner's Insurance Deductible
Major Car Repair or Replacement
New Roof or Air Conditioning Unit
<u>+ Two Months Living Expenses</u>
<u>Total Emergency Cash Reserve</u>

As a double check, you can compare the dollar amount from this formula to the six months living expense number. I'd go with whichever one is higher just to be safe. When in doubt, have more cash.

Federal Taxation: Unlimited Wants and Limited Resources

Threat #2 - Poor Tax Planning: It never ends. It seems like every time politicians talk about "simplifying taxes" they either *raise* them or add another thousand pages to the Tax Code. You get taxed on just about everything from your paycheck to gas for your car, electricity in your home, TV, Internet, phone, clothing, beer, wine, cigarettes, cars, boats, and houses. So, in other words, almost everything is taxed except breathing and groceries (at least not yet). To add to this, every form of city, county, state, and federal government has its hand in your pocket!

So where's the threat? With so much taxation already, we need to make sure that we don't do anything that will accidentally cause even more taxation. We need to make sure that we plan our finances to minimize taxes (unless you believe you don't pay enough in taxes . . . if that's the case, just send an extra check in with your next income tax return).

What's the fix? Here are some smart, and not-so-smart, tax moves:

Retirement-Smart Tax Moves to Consider

- Converting All or Part of Your Traditional IRA to a Roth IRA
- *Maxing Out* a Lower Income Tax Bracket
- Incurring Capital Gains Before Rates Are Expected to Go Up
- Using Lower Turnover Mutual Funds in Regular Brokerage Accounts and Higher Turnover Mutual Funds in IRAs

Not-So-Smart Tax Moves

- Getting a Home Mortgage Just for the Tax Deduction
- Taking Money from Your IRA to Pay Off Your Mortgage
- Taking Money Out of IRAs and Annuities Before Age 59½
- Not Considering That Investments Get Reset to Current Values at Death, Which Usually Reduces Capital Gains

Who Wants to Play *Monkey in the Middle*?

Threat # 3 - Long-term Care Expenses: Advances in medicine have extended life expectancy, but not necessarily the quality of our lives. Many of us will require some form of home health care or nursing home care during our lifetimes, and it won't be cheap. You may have already seen the huge costs involved if a member of your family has received such care. Thirty to fifty thousand dollars a year for assisted living or nursing home care is common; sixty or more is not unusual.

So where's the threat? If you have between $100,000 and $2,000,000 in financial assets, you need to take deliberate steps *now* to address the financial risks of long-term care so it doesn't wreck your retirement later.

What's the fix? If you have few financial resources, there is no threat. Well, actually, there is a threat, but it may not make any sense to do anything about it. In general, I've advised those who have less than $100,000 in financial assets to simply ignore the costs of long-term care. Why? In these situations, the costs of acquiring adequate long-term care insurance can be too high for their income and assets (why worry about the costs of what might or might not happen when it's possible there won't be enough money to pay the light bill?). Yes, I said ignore it, because if long-term care is required, those high costs would quickly deplete the available resources anyway and then the care is usually paid for by Medicaid, a government-funded safety net for the poor.

On the other hand, if you have substantial financial assets, say over $2,000,000, you could probably pay for long-term care costs out of your income or investment earnings. However, I would still investigate long-term care insurance for my clients who fit in this category.

If you've got hundreds of thousands but not millions of dollars, you're the *monkey in the middle* (just like in the grade school game). You've got enough money that you don't want to spend all of it to qualify for Medicaid, but not enough to ignore the potential costs of long-term care. That means you'll need some form of long-term care insurance. Ask an independent agent to help you find the best insurance for your individual financial situation. "Independent" means the agent doesn't represent just one insurance company and can help you compare products and solutions.

Sins of the Father and the Daughter

<u>**Threat # 4 - Family Financial Support**</u>: I offer my apologies in advance on this threat because I know it is a subject that will hit too close to home for some, literally. I'm not going to tell you to disown your family or that you shouldn't spoil the grandkids whenever you get the chance. I am very concerned, however, that you could jeopardize your own financial health while trying to help a family member with severe financial problems.

So where's the threat? They say a drowning person is dangerous and that you shouldn't put yourself at risk when offering aid. This is so true, both *in and out of the water*. This threat to your finances is, ironically, that your *love* for the person will cause you to make emotionally-driven bad choices that will hurt your own financial well-being and may even cause you to suffer the same *financial drowning* yourself.

First Example: I've watched a retired couple ruin their own finances by supporting a son who has a drug addiction. After *years* of second chances and promises of "I'll never do it again," the parents' good intentions have left them with very few financial resources. Their once healthy retirement savings have been replaced with second mortgages and skeletal investment accounts. Instead of letting their son hit bottom, go bankrupt and maybe change his ways, the parents now face financial doom themselves. A forty-year-old son can rebuild his finances, but a seventy-year-old father has few options to replenish his retirement.

Second Example: The threat of family financial support isn't just about parents supporting their kids. I once saw a daughter expend a huge portion of her and her husband's finances to provide long-term care for her parents. Most of us would consider this an honorable act, but the generosity forced the husband to work ten years longer than he planned.

What's the fix? Offer them your emotional support. Help them with the basics: food, clothing, and shelter. Help them apply for governmental programs. Explore bankruptcy if necessary. However, do not give them <u>more than 5% of your savings</u>. If it takes more than that to fix their problems, you probably don't have enough resources to help without putting yourself at risk. How can you help them if you are *caught in the rip current* yourself? Set the 5% financial gift limit and don't budge an inch.

Threat # 5 - Insufficient Survivor Income at the Death of a Spouse: With the average wife living about four years longer than the average husband, there is a significant chance that many women will end up handling their own finances. Of course, there are plenty of times when the situation is reversed, and the man finds himself on his own.

So where's the threat? When either spouse dies, retirement income is often reduced. The survivor must make do on one social security check, and perhaps, less pension income. The threat is that the survivor's solo income will be reduced to the point that her or his retirement assets must be drawn upon at an unsustainable rate. That means, at some point, the survivor could run out of money.

What's the fix? I am pleased to report that many couples *do* recognize that their finances will change when one of them dies. Often this leads to the wise decision to get help and develop a plan to understand exactly what could happen and how to deal with it. Of course, this kind of work is probably best done by an experienced adviser. I highly recommend that a couple build their financial plan so it will work while they are both alive, as well as in a survivorship scenario. While assisting retirees with their financial plans, I usually focus on making sure that enough reliable income will be provided to the spouse who would be more adversely affected by the death of her/his partner. In practical terms, this usually means that some financial changes may need to be made immediately. Here are some examples:

- The amount of life insurance may need to be increased.
- Long-term care costs will need to be addressed.
- Accounts may need to be "earmarked" for the survivor's needs.
- Investments may need to be more conservative or aggressive.
- The amount of joint income being taken may need to be reduced.
- More income may be needed from a guaranteed, fixed source.

The best time to do survivorship income planning, of course, is while both spouses are alive. This approach avoids the obvious difficulty of having to make financial decisions during a period of grief. Both spouses can feel confidence in the wisdom of an advanced plan for the survivor.

You Can't Get Milk Tomorrow from the Cow You Eat Today.

Threat # 6 - Excessive Withdrawal Rate: Here's an obvious statement: if you take too much from your investments and savings, you will run out of money. I've had the unpleasant task of telling some retirees that they were taking too much income from their portfolios. I delivered the bad news not because I like telling people "no" or that they "can't afford it," but to keep them from running out of money in the middle of their retirement. Some financial folks may say you can draw 4 to 6% a year and not run out of money in retirement. I say that's pure bologna and here's why:

- The typical retiree has a lot of fixed expenses. If you are drawing 6% from a $300,000 investment portfolio, you are taking $18,000 to pay your expenses. If your portfolio's value were to drop to $250,000, then that same 6% is just $15,000. I simply don't believe that the majority of retirees can slash their expenses so easily (and I don't think they should have to either). Most will still need the $18,000.

- A fixed 6% withdrawal rate also doesn't necessarily provide any inflation protection, unless your investment account is growing rapidly. To the contrary, you can actually experience a reduction in income when using a constant 6% withdrawal rate.

- While inflation will vary each year, we should budget for at least a 3% increase to have a realistic long-term plan for income.

- Moreover, drawing 6% from your investment portfolio can cause severe erosion to your portfolio's value during extended downturns in the market. Take the recent ten-year period of 2000 through 2009 as an example. Lets' start with the same $300,000 portfolio and run it through the actual returns for this period. We'll use the S&P 500 index for the hypothetical earnings, assuming dividends are reinvested. Additionally, we will assume a 2% annual asset management fee which decreases the index returns by 2%. (Take a look at the "Ending Value" on the following *Fairy Tale* chart). Who would have the bravado to stick with such a risky scheme when their portfolio falls by over 50% in the first three years? Nobody I know. How about you?

The *Fairy Tale* of a 6% Withdrawal Rate

Year	Earnings Including Dividends	Beginning Value	Withdrawal with a 3% Inflation Rate	Net Invested After Withdrawal	Investment Earnings	Ending Value
2000	-11.1%	300,000	18,000	282,000	(31,302)	250,698
2001	-13.9%	250,698	18,540	232,158	(32,247)	199,911
2002	-24.1%	199,911	19,096	180,815	(43,578)	137,237
2003	26.7%	137,237	19,669	117,568	31,373	148,941
2004	8.9%	148,941	20,259	128,682	11,429	140,111
2005	2.9%	140,111	20,867	119,244	3,471	122,715
2006	13.8%	122,715	21,493	101,222	13,963	115,185
2007	3.5%	115,185	22,138	93,047	3,252	96,299
2008	-39.0%	96,299	22,802	73,497	(28,663)	44,834
2009	24.5%	44,834	23,486	21,348	5,223	26,571

* Performance of the S&P 500 index includes reinvestment of dividends and a 2% annual asset management fee which decreases the index performance by 2% per year. Additional expenses, such as custodial fees and brokerage commissions, have not been considered, and if applied, would lower the return results. The Standard & Poor's 500 (S&P 500) is an unmanaged index commonly used to measure performance of U.S. stocks. S&P 500 consists primarily of large-capitalization stocks and may not be representative of a typical investor portfolio during retirement. You cannot invest directly into the S&P 500. The eighteen thousand dollar withdrawal is conservatively taken at the beginning of each year before applying the index annual return.

So where's the threat? This one's easy. If 6% is too much to withdraw annually, then you definitely cannot take more than 6%. If you take too much, you will run out. It is that simple. As the $26,571 ending value in 2009 screams, the damage can be irreparable. Sometimes waiting only makes things worse.

What's the fix? First, get a plan with realistic income projections that include inflation. Second, don't invest too much directly in the stock market. Third, make sure that a significant portion of your retirement income comes from fixed sources that don't depend on what the stock market does each year.

<u>Threat #7 - Unsustainable Lifestyle Spending</u>: Slow down. That's exactly what some people need to hear about their finances and lifestyle spending. These are usually the same people who hate the word, "budget." Hey, I understand; I can spend money as well as anyone. While you are working, you can get away with the occasional bouts of excessive spending because you have the time and the cash flow to replenish the deficit. However, when you stop working, your options shrink. You must make sure that your spending doesn't exceed your income.

So where's the threat? If your outflows exceed inflows, the difference has to come from either debt (such as credit cards, which is just delaying the problem) or from a reduction of your retirement assets (i.e., your investment principal). However, the more you reduce your investment principal, the greater the likelihood you'll run out of money. <u>That is a serious threat to your retirement</u>. A common source of stress among retirees (and arguments between spouses) is that they don't know how long their assets will last and how much they can draw each month.

What's the fix? Build a financial plan. Problem solved! A well-constructed financial plan is going to give you a year-by-year projection of how much consistent income your assets can provide. That income, after taxes of course, is what you get to spend! This is why I love planning for baby boomers and retirees. You can be more confident about what you can spend without running out! You can plan on that new kitchen, a new motorcycle, new cars, two rounds of golf a week, travel, vacations, addressing long-term care, fighting long-term inflation, and yes, even *bouncing that check to the undertaker* (well, not really, but you can decrease the likelihood of leaving a windfall to anyone when you die).

While I don't presume to be a relationship counselor, I have worked with hundreds of retirees, many of whom were couples. From this experience (and with apologies to Dr. Phil), I will say that spousal harmony seems to increase proportionally with financial certainty. More prudent spouses seem to relax once they know that they're not going to run out of money and more carefree spouses are happier because they get to spend and have fun, which is what they want anyway. Planning can be good for your finances and can be very good for your marriage. Don't fight. Get a plan.

Threat #8 - Trying to Use Dollar-Cost-Averaging in Retirement: Dollar-cost-averaging is a commonly used investment strategy where someone consistently invests a set dollar amount on a regular basis. Millions of working Americans do it with payroll-deducted contributions to 401(k) accounts. By investing, say a fixed $100 each month, investors buy more stock or mutual fund shares when the stock market is lower than when it is higher. If this strategy is used over a long period of time, there is an opportunity to get a lower average investment purchase price, which means less is paid for more shares. That means more profit when the stock market goes up. In other words, when the price of investments goes up, we buy fewer shares; when the price goes down, we buy more. It is like automatically buying more of something when it goes on "sale." Dollar-cost-averaging is considered by many to be a prudent investment strategy when saving for retirement.

So where's the threat? Things can go seriously wrong if you try to use dollar-cost-averaging when you are retired. When you start taking money out for retirement income, dollar-cost-averaging becomes risky because you may have to liquidate more of your investments when stock prices are lower to get the same monthly income. Look back a few pages at the **Fairy Tale of a 6% Withdrawal Rate** and recall what can happen to retirement savings if dollar-cost-averaging is used in retirement. The impact on savings can be devastating if the stock market suffers a sustained downturn. What was helpful dollar-cost-averaging during the accumulation years, becomes a dangerous tactic in the retirement years that can ravage a portfolio… so I call it *Dollar-Cost-Ravaging.*

What's the fix? Don't withdraw your monthly income from funds invested directly in the stock market or investments that can go down in value. I routinely recommend that retirees draw their income from investments and financial products where there is little or no risk of having to sell at a loss. I prefer stocks with high dividends, bonds for interest, and fixed annuities for a steady, reliable flow of income. Your personal circumstances and current conditions will determine what is best for you.

Every Year You Need More Money to Buy the Same Stuff.

Threat #9 – High Inflation: Inflation is often defined as the percentage increase in the price of goods and services from one year to the next. A 3% inflation rate means that $100 worth of stuff this year would cost $103 next year. A modest amount of inflation has long been considered acceptable in a growing economy. In fact, a small amount of inflation can even help to ease economic recessions and reduce the real level of debt.

The long-term average inflation rate in the United States for the last fifty years (1960 through 2009) has been about 4% as documented at inflationdata.com. Of course, averages can be very misleading. The highest single year of inflation during this fifty-year period occurred in 1980 with a whopping 13.58%! The lowest year was 2009 when inflation was flat (actually it was a year of slight deflation with prices falling about 1/3 of 1% from 2008).

So where's the threat? This one won't surprise you. What if your retirement years included a period of high inflation? Let's say you had retired at the end of 1978. The next three years produced a staggering total inflation of 35%! Just a few years into retirement and you could have seen a loss of 1/3 of your purchasing power! Are you cringing? I am. What if this kind of inflation happens again? *Now* are you cringing? I still am.

What's the fix? For the same three-year period of 1979, 1980, and 1981 which produced that 35% total inflation rate, the stock market racked up a cumulative gain of about 45%. Interesting, huh? Of course, it doesn't always work this way, nor should we expect *prior performance to be necessarily indicative of future results. Actual results can and will vary; you may incur a profit or loss* (yes, that is the common disclaimer). My point is that the stock market has historically been a good hedge against inflation.

With that said, it could be a good strategy to keep <u>some</u> of your retirement assets invested in the stock market after you retire. A diversified, low-cost, and professionally managed portfolio is one way to do that. However, most people shouldn't keep all of their money in the stock market. To avoid stress and uncertainty, retirees need preservation of principal, predictable income, and protection against inflation!

At Least They Aren't Charging You to Hold Your Money.

Threat # 10 - Low Interest Rates: Low interest rates are supposed to spur economic growth. Borrowing is cheaper for businesses and good for expansion. Low mortgage rates often lead to more home sales. More home sales are good for the economy. Growth is good.

So where's the threat? During low interest rate environments, many retirees have watched their interest incomes get cut in half. Unfortunately, nobody comes along and cuts retirees' expenses in half. That is the threat of a low interest rate scenario: incomes are reduced but expenses are not.

I used to mow my grandmother's yard when I was twelve. That was 1980. When I finished, I got $5, a *Little Debbie* snack cake, and a finance lesson. I will always remember sitting with my grandmother at her kitchen table as she explained how and why she put her money in CDs. She was earning about 14% at that time. All that interest sure seemed like a lot of money to me back then.

Today's interest rates are certainly a long way from that shimmering 14%. Just the other day, I drove by a bank sign that proudly displayed their eighteen month CD rate of 1.48%! Oh, how we long for those 14% interest rates again. Life would be so much easier, right? It is easy to overlook the fact that inflation was 13.6% in 1980. So, if we subtract inflation of 13.6% from that 14% interest, we get a real rate of return of just 1/2%. Math on some more recent interest and inflation numbers produces a similar result: 1.48% interest minus zero inflation in 2009 produces a real rate of return of about one and 1/2%. This more recent real rate of interest is low, but surprisingly, it is a little *higher* than the glorious 14% when you deduct inflation. I realize this math exercise doesn't solve the problem, but it is important to keep some perspective when we long for days gone by.

What's the fix? What is the purpose of accounts that are earning a low rate? Is it a cash reserve? Is it to provide income? Is it to protect principal? Better alternatives exist. However, some of these solutions may not be found at the local bank, may not be recommended in *Money Magazine*, or endorsed by the *WallStreet Journal.* An independent financial adviser can give you some fresh perspective on your alternatives.

You Can't Just Bury Your Money in the Backyard.

<u>Threat # 11 - Institution Failure</u>: Over the years, I've known a few people who became so distrusting of our financial system that they put their money into silver ingots and gold bars! The U.S. stock market meltdown and global financial crisis of 2008 probably had a lot of people considering this extremely defensive strategy. When economic uncertainty increases, people worry that the financial institutions that hold their assets will fail. I call this the risk of **institutional failure**, and it *is* one of the threats to retirement security.

Many Americans hold a large portion of their retirement assets in a variety of financial institutions, including banks and credit unions, insurance companies, and investment custodians. It is these institutions that people get concerned about when the economy is shaky. Of course, people also keep their financial resources in other places as well.

So where's the threat? Financial assets only have value because our financial system places a value on them. A stock certificate only has value because it is recognized by the overall financial system as representing ownership in a company. You cannot completely eliminate risk from a financial system. Even though it could be very small or remote, there will always be some risk. And if the whole financial system collapses, there is not much an individual investor can do about that. So our goal should be to minimize the risk of financial assets being lost due to the failure of individual institutions. How do we do that?

What's the fix? Check out the institutions where you put your money, preferably before you invest or open an account. Here are some Internet sites for checking the ratings and financial health of institutions:

- Banks: www.fdic.gov
- Credit Unions: www.ncua.gov
- Insurance Companies: www.ambest.com/consumers
- Investment Custodians: www.finra.org

Of course, if you are getting help from a financial adviser, it is his or her job to research and recommend financially stable and reputable companies.

Threat # 12 – Investment Losses: A real life story will illustrate the serious threat of investment losses. A retired couple came to me in 2007 for advice about their portfolio. They had amassed $500,000 through a lifetime of hard work, sacrifice, and savings. Their investments had also benefited nicely from the stock market gains of 2003 through 2007. They asked me to review their finances and to help them get retirement income from their portfolio. The wife had urged her husband to meet because she was nervous about all of their money being in the market. If the stock market did collapse, she wanted to make sure that their retirement lifestyle would be protected. After a thorough analysis of their investment holdings, I identified some problem areas. Of primary concern, 100% of their portfolio was invested in just a handful of *high octane* mutual funds that were rather aggressively invested in the stock market. I made recommendations on how they could enjoy income from their portfolio, substantially lower their risk of investment losses, and still have the opportunity for continued growth. Unfortunately, the husband would hear none of it. (When it comes to making logical financial decisions, we can be our own worst enemy.) *Intoxicated* by dreams of endless portfolio growth, he would not agree to the changes that would have provided a high probability of sustainable retirement income and better protection against a stock market downturn.

In 2008, I received a call. Their aggressive $500,000 portfolio had plummeted to just $250,000. As you might expect, I suggested that there were still ways that they could create retirement income and achieve better financial security with the remaining $250,000, but the husband could not see anything but a $250,000 loss. His greed had now been replaced by deep despair and paralyzing regret. (If this sounds like your situation, please don't give up! There is still plenty that can be done.)

What's the fix? While the stock market delivered a healthy average annual return of 12.8% from 1980 to 2009 (based on the S&P 500), it did so with returns ranging from a glorious gain of 38% in 1995 to a nasty loss of 37% in 2008. Money invested in individual stocks or growth mutual funds should not be money you are depending on for retirement income. Why? You may have to wait for the stock market to recover from a downturn before you can get your original investment back.

Innocent Mistakes Versus Bad Advice

<u>Threat #13 – Bad Advice</u>: Sound financial advice can be very helpful to investors in reaching their financial and retirement goals. However, advisers can make mistakes, and usually out of ignorance, can give bad advice. Bad advice is not the same thing as a financial scam.

So where's the threat? The best, most experienced advisers can still make mistakes. No one is perfect. Fortunately, financial errors or mistakes aren't as serious a threat because many times they can be corrected by an honest financial professional. The real threat comes from bad financial advice and from financial scams.

Bad advice can occur when an adviser, usually out of ignorance, recommends a product, investment, or strategy that is wrong for the client. Difficulties also arise when an adviser does not have the latitude to recommend the best financial product or investment because of a restrictive employment arrangement. If an adviser can recommend only one company, is that bad advice? No. It is selling and not advice at all.

A bad advice scenario: "Hank," a seventy-year-old divorced man, needs $20,000 a year from his $400,000 investment account to supplement his retirement income. His accounts are currently invested 100% in the stock market; all $400,000 is invested in about 75 individual stocks. Some of the stocks pay dividends, many do not. He will need to draw the $20,000 supplemental income each year whether the stock market is doing well or not. He is mostly concerned about outliving his money and inflation. He is not very concerned about leaving a large inheritance. Remember the *Fairy Tale* from a few pages back? In this case, I think the adviser gave this investor bad advice by putting all his money into the stock market. With the current investment strategy, our seventy-year-old could run out of money quickly with just a few years of poor stock market performance.

What's the fix? Better advice would be to give Hank a portfolio without so much risk. Yes, that would take more time; it might involve multiple accounts; it might require both stock market investments as well as fixed income products, but that is what financial and retirement planning is all about. That's the financial adviser's job. Advisers should provide customized financial solutions, not a one-size-fits-all formula.

What Million Dollar Account?!

Threat # 14 - Financial scams: Scams occur when a person (financial adviser or otherwise) attempts to steal an investor's money or to get the investor to buy an investment of some type through misrepresentation, lying, and/or manipulation. By gaining control of the victim's investment funds, scams have been committed by a wide variety of perpetrators. Financial scams are usually more devastating than a simple mistake, or even bad advice, because of the perpetrator's intent: theft.

A story about financial scams: A few years ago a gentlemen in his late sixties, let's call him "Walter," came to me for a pre-retirement review of his finances. He wanted to make sure that he and his wife could retire comfortably on what they had accumulated. I was able to analyze all of his holdings, except for his largest account which he said was worth about a million dollars. The performance reports indicated that his account had averaged about 18% a year and had side-stepped most of the stock market's recent drops. Walter, understandably, was very proud of that performance. I was very curious to review the holdings of his account, but he only had partial statements, which made me suspicious. In order for me to analyze the account and determine how the adviser was generating such high performance results, I would need to see complete statements. I was concerned that a great deal of risk was being taken to achieve the high returns. I wasn't that far off.

Two months passed before Walter and I had another meeting. A large financial scam had been revealed in the newspaper, and he discovered that he had been one of the victims. Shockingly, he found out there was no million dollar account. That would certainly explain why he didn't get statements. Walter's retirement plans were destroyed over night. He will probably work the rest of his life.

What's the fix? The last I heard, Walter and a group of fellow victims were suing to recoup some of their losses. What a sad story. How do you protect yourself? Here are three simple steps:

1. Never write checks to a financial adviser.
2. Be suspicious if you don't get brokerage statements.
3. If it sounds too good to be true, it probably is. Run.

Would You *Ever* Get Your Car Repaired Without an Estimate?

Threat # 15 - High Investment Fees: One of the things I review when I give people *second opinions* on their finances is their investment fees. I continue to be amazed at how little most people understand about the cost of investments. The truth, however, is that it really isn't the investor's fault. The financial industry has done a poor job of disclosing and explaining investment costs. The industry's primary disclosure document about fees and how investments work is called a *prospectus*; many investors call it a "doorstop." Nobody reads it! Why? Because it is an inch thick, the type is hard to read without a magnifying glass, and the words are written *by attorneys for attorneys*. Given this reality, it is the financial adviser's job to help investors understand the fees they pay.

So where's the threat? The threat is that many people pay more than they realize for their investments. Let's say Tom has a $200,000 investment portfolio and for ten years he has been paying 1% more than he should have. That would mean Tom paid an extra $20,000 in fees!

Here's a real life story that will make my point: after attending one of my recent financial presentations, a woman asked me to review her investments. When I analyzed her account and expenses, I determined she was paying 3.8% each year on a $165,000 account. That's $6,270 in fees! Perhaps the investments were worth it? Cheaper isn't always better. Better is better. Unfortunately, there wasn't anything outstanding about her investments; they were just expensive. My biggest concern for her was that she had absolutely no idea what she was paying. It didn't need to be this way. I told her that she should consider some lower cost alternatives.

What's the fix? Incredibly, many people invest without ever knowing what they pay in fees. We would never tolerate cost ignorance in other parts of our life. When was the last time you dropped your car off for service and told them to fix whatever they wanted, regardless of the cost? I'll bet never. The fix for this threat is simple: do not buy any investment or financial products without clearly understanding all fees and expenses. Ask the adviser to disclose all fees in writing before you sign. If you are already invested and don't know what you are paying, get a second opinion from a qualified adviser. Do not settle for inadequate service or inadequate fee disclosure.

Dealing with the Threats

Once you have accumulated sufficient assets to retire, or if you are already retired, prudent stewardship of your financial resources should not end. While accumulation of retirement assets is commendable, there are ongoing responsibilities that must be met to make sure that none of these threats *pop* your retirement balloon.

Since the threats to a secure retirement are known, the key question is whether you will act wisely to keep them from disrupting your retirement dreams. A truly secure retirement is only possible when you make informed decisions about your money and when you take deliberate, specific steps to minimize any threats. To deal with the threats, proactive planning is needed.

When it comes to your personal finances and the pursuit of a secure retirement, there is no room for "political correctness" or sugar-coating. Thankfully, for you and me, you won't find any of those niceties in this book.

Secret #3: Don't Let Emotions Ruin Your Retirement

The U.S. stock market amassed a total return of 450% between 1991 and 1999. During the exuberance of the longest bull market in U.S. history, individual investors feasted on huge helpings of stock market growth. Investment losses seemed to be a thing of the distant past (you'd have to set your time machine to the year 1974 to find a calendar year when the stock market lost 10% or more). Many investors did not realize, or they simply didn't care, how much risk they were taking in the 1990's. In fact, I distinctly remember one very deluded TV pundit declaring:

"Diversification is dead. Why bother with asset allocation? Just put all your money in technology stocks."

With the luxury of hindsight, of course, everyone knows how ridiculous a statement this was, but it was not all that unusual at the time. Then, just a few months into 2000, *the bubble burst!* Many investors felt helpless as their portfolios hemorrhaged losses for three years. When the carnage finally ended in 2002, the stock market had lost 43% of its value. Investors had not seen such losses in over twenty-five years.

More recently, consider the stock market collapse of 2008. Old wounds were re-opened and new ones were inflicted on several generations of American investors. For many, the 37% market decline in 2008 didn't just drain them financially, but it depleted them emotionally as well.

These stock market declines caught many investors and financial advisers flat-footed without a strategy to deal with their losses. Investors panicked, advisors pulled their hair out, everyone blamed everyone else, and emotions ruled the day. Prudent planning was often abandoned. With the equivalent mental impairment of *five shots* of Tequila, otherwise intelligent people made very bad financial decisions.

So, why the history lesson you may ask? I have three key points for you:

1. Another market drop will come. The only question is "when?"
2. You can't let emotions drive your decision-making when it does.
3. A sound plan can help you keep your sanity during tough times.

It is time for another real life story. I always change the details enough to protect the person's privacy and to save them from any potential embarrassment. The story unfolds in 1999 and is still very relevant today. In 1999, "Mr. Jones" took all of his IRA money and bought one stock with it. He purchased 1,000 shares of a publicly-traded technology company. At that time, technology stocks in general were doing very well. In February of 1999, the stock was trading at $80 per share, so his total purchase price was $80,000.

Mr. Jones wanted to retire in a couple years. He knew that he had not been able to save enough for his retirement, but he hoped that the stock market's strong performance in 1999 would continue in the 2000s. He desperately hoped that his "all in gamble" with the one stock would be his golden ticket to a carefree retirement. He was 60 at the time and he really did not want to work until the normal retirement age of 65.

Incredibly, the stock rocketed from the purchase price of $80 a share to $641 a share by the end of 1999. By February 24th of 2000, the stock's after-burners had kicked in, and it reached a staggering $1,230 per share. His gamble had paid off beyond his wildest expectations. His early retirement was within sight. In less than a year, his $80,000 investment had grown to $1,230,000!

Since I am telling you his story, I must have met Mr. Jones at some point. Now, when do you think that happened? Was it when his IRA was worth $641,000? How about when it hit $1,230,000? Was that when he came in for advice? Unfortunately, not. Why didn't he come in when his IRA reached $1,230,000? Because at the time, many people, including Mr. Jones, thought the stock market would continue to soar into the stratosphere! Unbridled greed ran free. Next stop . . . the moon! No, make that Mars!

He finally came to see me in May of 2000, when his stock was plunging back to Earth (like a lot of stocks at the time). His IRA was now "only" worth $512,000. After hearing his story, I expected him to ask how he could diversify, protect what he had left, or create an income stream from his IRA. However, believe it or not, that was not what he wanted to know.

"You only find out who is swimming naked when the tide goes out." - Warren Buffet

Mr. Jones just wanted to know one thing, "When's the stock going to go back up?" I'm not kidding. It is funny now, but it was awfully sad at the time. Of course, by now, you know what I told him, "Number one, I have no idea what the stock will do. Number two, if you want to retire in a year, you'd better sell the stock now and diversify. Number three, it'd be real smart to take some money off the table and put it into safer investments that provide reliable income. And, number four, let's build a written financial plan so you can retire with confidence."

Obviously, Mr. Jones would have done very well if he had cashed-in his stock when it was worth $1,230,000, but he wouldn't do that. I think for him and for many people, it would have been better if the stock had never gone any higher than the $512,000 value. The $1,230,000 distorted his perspective.

The Rise and Fall of Mr. Jones

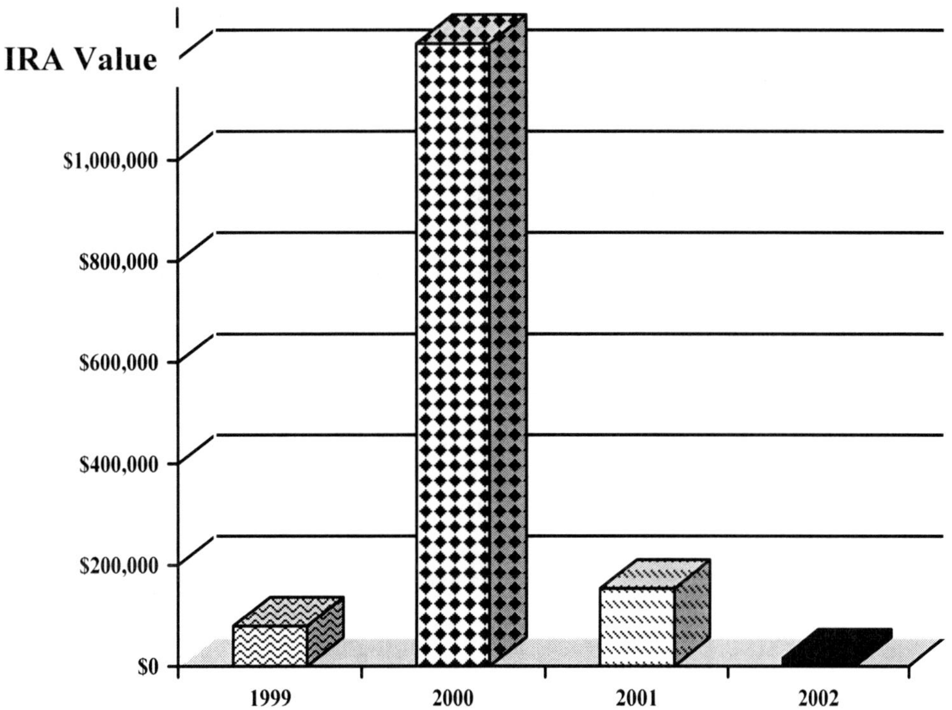

Whatever Happened to Mr. Jones?

Unfortunately, logical advice was not what Mr. Jones wanted to hear. He couldn't hear or see anything but a $700,000 loss of value from February 24th to May 5th in 2000. He could no longer see that he had, in fact, made $430,000 on his original $80,000 investment in just one year. Mr. Jones left my office on May 5th, 2000 frustrated by my advice to sell the stock for $512,000. I truly believe he knew he had made a serious mistake. I think he just wanted someone to validate his poor judgment. So, I encouraged him to give his finances more thought, and I asked him to come back when he was ready to do some realistic retirement planning.

It took about two more weeks, and another $80,000 in losses, for Mr. Jones to surrender to the wisdom of getting out of the stock and getting into a financial plan. On May 18th, 2000, Mr. Jones reluctantly agreed to sell his stock, then worth $438,000. Thank God. The stock's value continued to implode. By December 31st, 2000, it had fallen to $154 per share. Two years later on December 31st, 2002, the stock closed at $16 a share. By December 31st, 2009, it was worth a measly $2.13 a share.

I have a special message for those who subscribe to the investment philosophy, "I won't sell at a loss no matter what." My response is simple, "What do you think Mr. Jones would say?" Where would he be today if he had been *bull-headed* and refused to ever sell at a loss? I can tell you precisely where he'd be...he'd have a stock worth $2,130 and a lousy retirement. I know for a fact that Mr. Jones' retirement is much better today because he wised up and sold the falling stock. A wounded pride and $438,000 in cash are far better than $2,130 shrouded in a fortress of self-delusion.

Strategy Action Item

I call the emotional decision-making we've discussed the "Casino Effect," because it is awfully hard to get up from the blackjack or roulette table when you are down. You feel like you have to at least break even before you stop. Then, when you start winning, you can't stop because *you're on a roll!* Free drinks while you are playing, no clocks on the walls...sounds a lot like investing in the stock market, doesn't it? Please don't let your emotions get in the way of sound planning for you and your family.

Secret #4: Live Long and Prosper (by Planning Well)

How long you expect to live will have a big impact on how you plan your retirement. According to the infoplease.com website (accessed February 23, 2011), human life expectancy was just forty-seven years in 1900. More recent data from the CIA's World Factbook puts life expectancy in the United States at 75.8 for men and 80.8 for women (www.cia.gov, accessed February 23, 2011). For an even more relevant planning perspective, I think we should look at how life expectancy for 60-year-olds has increased over the last 100 years (I created this chart using historical data accessed from www.infoplease.com on April 15th, 2011).

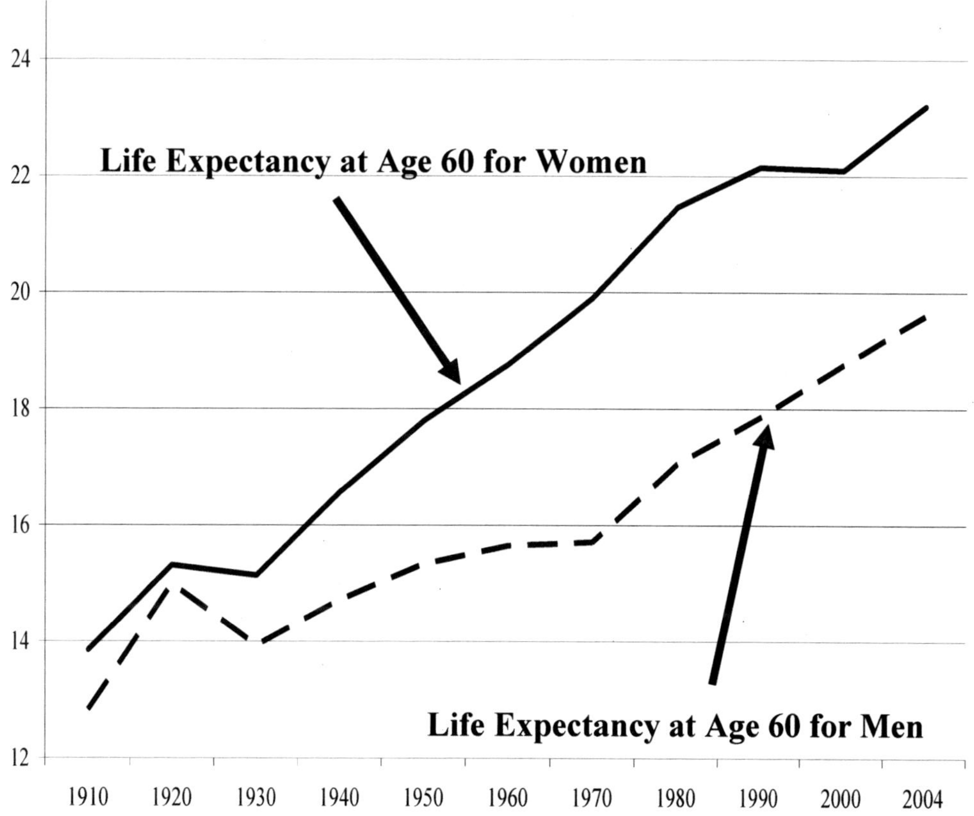

This more recent statistic of life expectancy for 60-year-olds provides useful information we need for retirement planning. **In 2004, the average 60-year-old woman was expected to live 23 years to age 83. The average 60-year-old man was expected to live about 19 years to age 79.**

Don't Fear the Reaper. It is Longevity That Can Be the Death of You.

What does this clarity about individual longevity mean for retirement planning? If a 60-year-old woman is in good health, makes good lifestyle choices, and has a history of longevity in her family, she could live to 100.

If she were to retire at 60, she might need retirement income for a whopping 40 years! She certainly shouldn't deplete all her assets by age 83. If she lives to 100, she would need income for 17 years longer than the average 60-year-old woman. In fact, depending on her financial resources and income needs, she might even need to put off retirement. Delaying retirement would allow her assets to grow and would also shorten the period during which she would need retirement income. Prudent planning would be crucial to her reaching 100 with money still in the bank.

Your family history of longevity and your personal health directly affect how long you will live. Your lifestyle choices also make a difference (such as whether you smoke, how much alcohol and coffee you drink, and whether you jump out of perfectly good airplanes). If you've ever applied for life insurance, you know that insurance company actuaries care about these factors, so the underwriters ask a bunch of personal questions. If the insurance company doesn't think you are going to live as long as the "average," then, you guessed it, they are going to charge you a higher premium for the same life insurance coverage.

To help you think about your own longevity and the length of time your retirement assets will need to provide income, a helpful longevity calculator created by Dr. Thomas Perls can be found at:

www.livingto100.com.

Thomas Perls, M.D. is Assistant Professor of Medicine, Harvard Medical School, a geriatrician at Beth Israel Deaconess Medical Center, and co-authored the book, *Living to 100.*

Double Check Before You Tell Your Boss What You *Really* Think

Because of increasing longevity, the need for money to last longer, and poor investment results, the grim reality for many pre-retirees is that they will need to work longer than they originally planned. It hasn't made me very popular when I have given someone a financial "reality check" and told them that they need to work longer. I'll take the "heat," because I know that my **financial 2nd opinions** will help these soon-to-be retirees reduce the risk of outliving their retirement resources. The obvious question people need to ask themselves is, "how do we know if we need to wait?" While there's no magical formula, there are facts we'll need in order to make a proper assessment. Here are some questions I'd ask:

- How large is your available lump sum?
- How much are your social security and pensions?
- What are your other sources of income?
- What is your desired total amount of retirement income?

With this information, we can determine if the lump sum is big enough to meet the desired goals. For example, if a person has $400,000 saved for retirement, but their goals require $500,000, then we're $100,000 short. As they say, "something's gotta give." Either the retirement date needs to be delayed (so a bigger lump sum can accumulate) or retirement income needs to be reduced (so the lump sum will last longer). It is that simple.

Of course, if you are already retired, a discussion about how long you need to work doesn't make much sense unless you find out that you need to go back to work. So, how do you know whether or not you are even on the right financial path? I recommend that retirees verify that they are on track by getting a **financial 2nd opinion** from an experienced financial adviser.

Over the years, I've helped hundreds of retirees plan their financial futures. Too often, I've seen situations where well-intending retirees have made serious mistakes that could have crippled their finances further down the retirement road. It is well worth your time and energy to have your retirement plan and investments reviewed to make sure you are doing what is right for your situation. Financial products and investments continue to evolve; you need to make sure you are taking advantage of the latest and best strategies available in the marketplace.

Changing the Tires on the Car While You Are Still in the Race

A **financial 2nd opinion** can help you identify whether you are making any of the common mistakes that I've seen retirees make during my financial career, which include:

- Disregarding the benefits of a written, coordinated financial plan
- Investing too heavily in the stock market
- Drawing retirement income from the stock market
- Paying too much in investment fees
- Withdrawing too quickly from retirement savings for income
- Ignoring the need for survivorship income
- Failing to address the costs associated with long-term care

These mistakes can cause financial pain and hardship, but all of them can be avoided. Armed with a better knowledge of your situation from the financial 2nd opinion, you can take corrective action such as:

- Changing your investment strategy or individual holdings
- Shifting to a more conservative overall approach
- Establishing a guaranteed source of retirement income
- Setting aside funds to address long-term care expenses
- Spending money to get your estate planning documents in order
- Reducing the income you take from your accounts
- Changing financial advisers or firing your broker
- Putting your retirement on hold and going back to work

If you need to make some significant (or even unpleasant) changes to your finances, it is so much better to do that now, rather than to go forward blindly, not knowing that you should have taken action sooner.

Strategy Action Item

When you build a retirement income plan, it is absolutely critical that the income it provides will last as long as you do, even if you live longer than you expect. Income should take into account inflation, be as certain as possible, and not be based on *pie-in-the-sky* assumptions.

Secret #5: Dollar-Cost-Ravaging Only Works in the Movies

The typical male has a better chance of winning a comparison to *Prince Charming* in the standard *girls-night-out-chic-flick* than *dollar-cost-ravaging* has of providing a lifetime of retirement income. And, men, you know our odds are not good!

Sadly, I have seen too many investors get hurt by *dollar-cost-ravaging.* I am hoping to put an end to this risky investment scheme, right here and right now (at least for you), so here we go. What was *dollar-cost-ravaging* again? It is taking systematic withdrawals from an investment portfolio in order to provide income (say, $500 a month). Withdrawals come from the money invested in the stock market, regardless of whether there are profits or losses. Now, you are probably asking yourself, "if it is so dangerous, and if it doesn't work, why would someone try to do it?" I'll answer that question this way: the other day I saw a woman driving a car with a dog in her lap. She had her cell phone in one hand and a hamburger in the other! Just because it's dangerous doesn't mean some people aren't going to do it! Here are several reasons why I believe some people take chances with *dollar-cost-ravaging*:

- Bad Financial Advice: surprisingly, many financial advisers do not understand the risks associated with this approach to income.

- Narrow Adviser Capabilities: some advisers may be limited, or even encouraged by their employment arrangements, to keep their clients in all securities or stock market positions (instead of using guaranteed and safer fixed-income alternatives).

- Investor Ignorance: some investors have invested successfully using dollar-cost-averaging during their working years and don't realize they need to make a conservative shift in their retirement years.

- Investor Desperation: they know they don't have enough retirement funds saved, but they still need the income. They are praying for a miracle, or at least some good luck, to make it work.

- Investor Greed: for some, there will never be enough accumulated.

12.8% Return . . . Well, Hellooooooo Gorgeous!

Here's a hypothetical example that may help you understand what goes on in some people's minds. With an original investment of $300,000, this hypothetical couple would be able to enjoy $446,000 of income and still have over $432,000 left over in their investment account. However, what you see in the chart below has never happened, and it likely never will.

Year	Annual Return	Client Age	Client Age	Beginning Value	Account Growth	2% Fee	Income with 3% Inflation	Ending Value
1	12.8%	61	61	300,000	38,400	6,288	24,000	308,112
2	12.8%	62	62	308,112	39,438	6,457	24,720	316,374
3	12.8%	63	63	316,374	40,496	6,628	25,462	324,780
4	12.8%	64	64	324,780	41,572	6,803	26,225	333,324
5	12.8%	65	65	333,324	42,665	6,980	27,012	341,997
6	12.8%	66	66	341,997	43,776	7,159	27,823	350,791
7	12.8%	67	67	350,791	44,901	7,341	28,657	359,695
8	12.8%	68	68	359,695	46,041	7,524	29,517	368,694
9	12.8%	69	69	368,694	47,193	7,710	30,402	377,775
10	12.8%	70	70	377,775	48,355	7,896	31,315	386,919
11	12.8%	71	71	386,919	49,526	8,084	32,254	396,107
12	12.8%	72	72	396,107	50,702	8,272	33,222	405,316
13	12.8%	73	73	405,316	51,880	8,460	34,218	414,518
14	12.8%	74	74	414,518	53,058	8,647	35,245	423,685
15	12.8%	75	75	423,685	54,232	8,832	36,302	432,782

This chart represents what some people (and some advisers) expect when they keep 100% of their retirement money invested in stocks—and then try to draw lifetime income from the same. Why? Simple: the stock market really did produce a spectacular 12.8% average return for the thirty-year period of 1980 to 2009 (I'm talking about the S&P 500 index with dividends, but no taxes). People think that if the stock market provided that kind of return over such a long period of time, then they should be able to assume the same kind of return for their investments during their retirement years. The problem, of course, is that while the stock market has averaged 12.8%, it has never actually done so in such a smooth and pretty fashion. *How* and *when* you earn your gains is extremely important.

Danger, Will Robinson! Danger! Here Comes Reality!

Now let's take a look at the same fifteen-year chart as before with one simple change: the returns now vary each year. I've assumed both negative and positive returns, but the average annual return is still 12.8%. This looks a lot more like what we are used to seeing in the real world.

Year	Annual Return	Client Age	Client Age	Beginning Value	Account Growth	2% Fee	Income with 3% Inflation	Ending Value
1	0.0%	61	61	300,000	-	5,520	24,000	270,480
2	6.0%	62	62	270,480	16,229	5,240	24,720	256,749
3	-12.0%	63	63	256,749	(30,810)	4,010	25,462	196,468
4	-12.0%	64	64	196,468	(23,576)	2,933	26,225	143,733
5	-12.0%	65	65	143,733	(17,248)	1,989	27,012	97,483
6	6.0%	66	66	97,483	5,849	1,510	27,823	74,000
7	24.0%	67	67	74,000	17,760	1,262	28,657	61,840
8	24.0%	68	68	61,840	14,842	943	29,517	46,222
9	24.0%	69	69	46,222	11,093	538	30,402	26,374
10	24.0%	70	70	26,374	6,330	28	31,315	1,362
11	24.0%	71	71					
12	24.0%	72	72	**Out of Money!**				
13	24.0%	73	73					
14	24.0%	74	74					
15	24.0%	75	75					

Although this fifteen-year period still has the average return of 12.8%, the results are now very different because of the (more realistic) negative returns in some years. In fact, it only takes three down years to cause our hypothetical retired couple to run out of money by year ten, despite 24% annual returns thereafter! Amazing, isn't it? The investment portfolio is never able to recover from the negative results in years three, four, and five, even with incredibly high performance later.

To illustrate how much damage was actually done, I've calculated that it would take an absurd 42% return each year for the next nine years in a row in order for the portfolio to provide the desired income for the full fifteen-year period. Even then, our hypothetical couple would still be out of money after fifteen years.

What exactly causes so much damage so quickly? The real culprit: withdrawals taken while the portfolio is experiencing negative stock market performance. Take a look at how much the ending value falls from the end of year two to the end of year five. The portfolio shrank a whopping $159,266 in just three years. $78,699 of that drop can be accounted for as withdrawals. Where did the rest go? Well, $8,932 went to fees, but that is not the problem. The rest of the money was lost due to selling investments to make withdrawals while the stock market was down. In this example, *dollar-cost-ravaging* had a hefty price: $71,634.

Now, some high-falutin' TV "stock market expert" reading this book might say: *"Well, yeah, but that's only because you're taking money out. This is really easy to fix. Whenever the market goes down, just don't take any money out. It isn't a loss unless you sell. Think long-term."*

On behalf of retirees everywhere, I would love to respond: *Really, that's your multi-million-dollar-TV-budget answer? Don't you realize that most retirees can't stop taking money out anytime they choose? Most have fixed expenses, so they need the steady income. Your solution is overly simplistic, out-of-touch, and impractical for most American retirees.*

Ways to Avoid *Dollar-Cost-Ravaging* That You Won't Hear on TV

- Carve out enough of your retirement assets to produce the income you need, and invest those funds in more secure places, such as:
    - Certificates of deposit and laddered bonds
    - An immediate annuity (create your own pension)
    - A deferred annuity with lifetime income guarantees

- Invest the remaining portion of your retirement assets in mutual funds and individual stocks to fight long-term inflation.

How much has *dollar-cost-ravaging* cost you? Can you remember a three-year period when the market fell? How long did it take for your portfolio to recover? Is it still recovering? Don't put your retirement security at risk by exposing all of your savings to stock market downturns. The time it takes to recover may be longer than the length of your retirement.

Secret #6: Gold, Guns, Chickens, and Inflation

I must confess that I've been frustrated at times when I've tried to help some retirees who've gotten sucked into the media's hyperbole and half-truths about financial doom and gloom. It's impossible to create a logical financial plan for someone who really thinks the world is about to end! Depending on which cable television shows you watch and which major political party is in power, you may hear that we are on the brink of disaster or a global economic meltdown. It seems modern TV "news" has morphed into an ugly cross between the Jerry Springer Show and Walter Cronkite! One of the new financial show formats is to have two diametrically opposed talking-heads scream at each other for ten minutes. I miss real journalism, don't you?

One of the financial threats that the media just *loves* to talk about is hyperinflation. Their "prognosticators" proclaim that we are "printing money like crazy," which will cause runaway inflation. I'm not saying we won't have some inflation, or maybe even high inflation, but I am just not convinced that it will be *out of control inflation.* If the United States were to ever experience *hyperinflation* or if the global economic system were to collapse, there might be no way to plan for it – except maybe to stock up on *shotguns and chickens*. You'll need the chickens to lay eggs so you can eat and a shotgun to keep other people from stealing your chickens! No amount of gold will help at that point. Gold: you can't eat it, you can't shoot it, and *my* eggs won't be for sale *no matter how much gold you've got*! So, please don't get reeled in by talk radio and TV pitchmen to buy gold coins, unless you really are a coin collector.

Gold is not the best inflation hedge. It is a crisis hedge. Whenever people have gotten scared about the financial system, they have looked to gold. I'm not here to bash gold as an investment. It is a commodity, and as such, it can be part of a well-diversified investment portfolio. If you want gold, let's put it in your portfolio through mutual funds and exchange-traded funds. Just don't bet the farm or your retirement on it!

Inflation is, by no means, dead. If we look at the fifty-year period of 1960 through 2009, **forty nine of those years had inflation**. 2009 was the only year without inflation. We actually had a smidgen of deflation (prices actually went down). The highest inflation was 13.6% in 1980 and the lowest was 1.6% in 1998. While history is not a predictor of the future, it would be certainly reasonable to expect that we will have inflation in the future, and inflation is likely to be high in some of those years.

What causes inflation?

Many things can cause inflation, including upward wage pressure and increases in commodity prices such as oil, food, industrial metals, and timber. Inflation can also occur when our government, through the Federal Reserve, increases the total amount of money in our financial system faster than our economy is growing. The money supply is increased in an effort to stimulate economic growth to get us out of a recession. Often, interest rates are also lowered to stimulate growth.

Page 2. Now, for the Rest of the "Inflation" Story.
(a small tribute to the late Paul Harvey, radio legend)

Is Inflation Bad?

A modest amount of inflation is actually considered by many financial experts to be healthy for economic growth. 2 to 3% seems to be the target range used by the Federal Reserve when setting interest rates and adjusting how much money is in our financial system. When inflation rises above the target range, the Federal Reserve usually steps in to slow the economic growth (by raising interest rates and/or by draining off some of the money supply). Inflation averaged 4.1% from 1960 to 2009. Anything above 5% per year gives the policy makers heartburn and is considered high inflation.

Should You Care about High Inflation?

Yes. Here's why:

- From 1979 to 1981, inflation was a whopping 35%. Let's say you are getting $1,200 from Social Security, and high inflation like that reoccurs in the next three years. Now your social security is only worth about $780.

- Businesses have to raise prices to get the same "value" for their products.

- Uncertainty about the future can cause people to take a "bunker" mentality. People become reluctant to invest, which isn't good for the economy or your stock market investments.

- There is pressure on wages to go up to keep pace with inflation; those higher wages are passed on to the consumer through higher prices, which causes more inflation.

What is Hyperinflation?

When "regular" inflation gets out of control and prices increase by 50% or more per year, that's hyperinflation. Historically, hyperinflation has been caused by rapid and large increases in a country's money supply without a corresponding growth in the economy. Lack of confidence in the value of the country's paper currency becomes widespread. Consumers avoid holding cash any longer than necessary to purchase goods and services.

Hyperinflation can ultimately lead to the abandonment of the currency in favor of a barter system, the use of precious metals (like gold), or the use of a foreign currency.

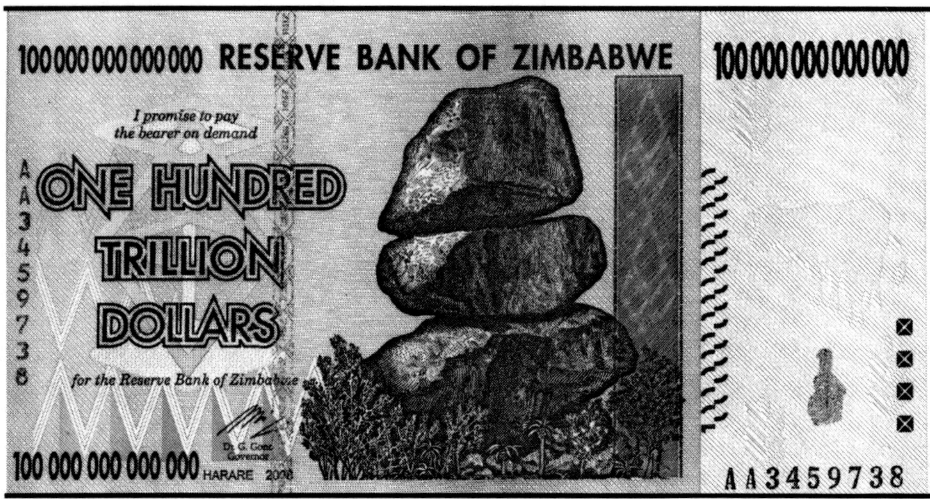

In the 2000s, a hyperinflation plague descended on the African nation of Zimbabwe. "Aggressive" land reforms and an economic upheaval collided with the unprecedented printing of money by the Zimbabwe government. In the end, wheel barrels of money were needed just to buy bread! Ultimately, the local currency was discontinued and foreign currencies, like the U.S. dollar, were used instead.

Now, the Zimbabwe One Hundred Trillion Dollar note is only worth what collectors are willing to pay for it. I paid $1.25 for this one on eBay.

Inflation Vaccination

While the likelihood of hyperinflation visiting the United States is remote, it is sound planning to protect your retirement from the effects of long-term "regular" inflation. One dollar today will only be worth about 69 cents after ten years of average inflation.

Average Annualized Growth Rates (1980 – 2009)

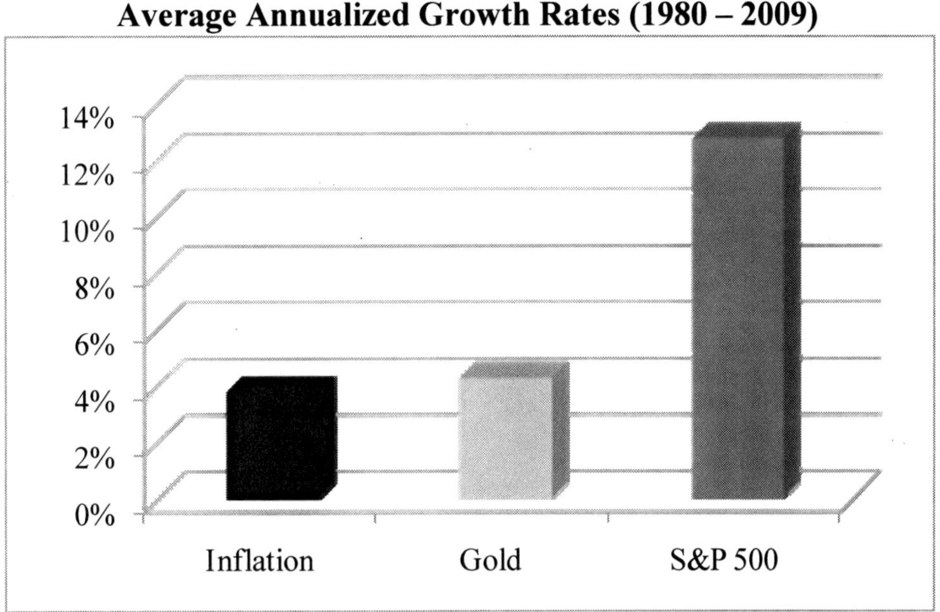

This graph compares the performance of gold and the stock market to inflation for 1980 through 2009. During this thirty-year period (ignoring expenses and taxes), inflation was up an average of 3.8%, gold glimmered an average return of 4.3%, and the S&P 500 index produced an average return of 12.8%.

Strategy Action Item

To vaccinate your finances against the ravages of long-term inflation, you'll want to consider having some of your assets invested for long-term growth. A little gold is okay. However, long-term, low-cost stock market investments may be a better choicc to fight inflation, but don't put all your money in one stock. Diversification has helped a lot more people than it has ever hurt, and it may help improve your returns over time.

Section II

The Planning Needed to Overcome the Threats

Secret #7: Do You Have Good Investments?

Good investments? What does that mean? Are they *good* because they are diversified? Does being safe make them *good*? Are they *good* because they made you a lot of money last year? They outperformed their peers, so does that make them *good*? The purpose of this chapter is to help you understand how to evaluate your investments and how to determine whether they are the right choices for you.

In my financial planning practice, we routinely prepare what we call our *19-Point Investment Inspection.* It is a financial analysis that focuses on the investor's current investment holdings and gauges the *goodness* of the client's financial assets using the following criteria:

1. Do the assets provide a valuable benefit for what the investor is paying? How much *bang for the buck* is the investor getting?
2. Are the assets appropriate for the investor's individual situation, needs, and goals? *Does the shoe fit?*

Most investment and financial products can be evaluated on this basis. It isn't difficult. It just takes time, the right tools, and a healthy dose of objectivity. To the surprise of many prospective clients and other financial advisers, my firm doesn't charge for this service. Why? Is it because we use it as a *loss-leader* or a gimmick? No, but I must confess that our *19-Point Investment Inspection* is as much a tool for us as it is for potential clients. The truth is that I simply cannot tell people what they should do with their money unless I first understand their current financial situation. To do otherwise would be like a mechanic telling someone he needs a new fan belt without ever lifting the hood. We need to roll-up our sleeves, raise the hood, and connect our computer to the engine to do our *Inspection.* We need to review investment statements, annuity policies, and other financial documents.

Of course, a thorough analysis takes some time (about a week). Our *Inspection* sometimes takes a little longer than some people can wait. One gentleman comes to mind; he expected us to just "go in the back" and grab some investments "off the shelf" like we were selling air filters! A step-by-step approach will take a little more time, but it is so worth it.

19-Point Investment Inspection

Over the years, I have found that these 19 points will address many of the investment "problem" areas, as well as the planning that needs to be done for a successful retirement. Is this everything that can be considered or analyzed? No. However, it is a good start. Here's the list:

1. Check if asset allocation is in line with financial goals
2. Determine whether there is adequate stock diversification
3. Identify any holdings over 5% of the portfolio and assess risk
4. Identify stock holdings over 1% of the portfolio and assess risk
5. Check the Morningstar rating for each holding
6. Identify any holdings with investment fees above 1.5%
7. Evaluate overall portfolio fees
8. Assess fixed annuity rates, riders, and costs
9. Assess variable annuity subaccounts, riders, and costs
10. Assess the quality of individual fixed income holdings
11. Determine if there is adequate bond diversification
12. Identify bond maturity and assess interest rate risk
13. Evaluate current bond yield versus maturity and credit ratings
14. Review plan for long-term care
15. Evaluate overall strategy for lifestyle funding
16. Evaluate overall strategy with survivorship scenario
17. Evaluate existing life insurance adequacy or necessity
18. Assess the portfolio's overall risk of *dollar-cost-ravaging*
19. Assess possible benefit of IRA to Roth IRA Conversion

As we get into each individual point of the analysis, please keep in mind that we will be looking at two key, distinct characteristics for most of them: first, *bang for your buck,* and second, *does the shoe fit?* Sometimes, this analysis will show that a particular investment or financial product is *good* because of the value it provides, but it may not be appropriate for the individual's situation (here's a good analogy: a gorgeous top grain leather shoe that is marked 50% off, but is too tight on that pinky toe – or we've already got four pairs in the same color). Our analysis may indicate the need to get rid of an investment even though it has performed well. As we go through each of the 19 points, I promise that this peculiarity will make more sense to you. So, slide on your coveralls, and let's go to work.

#1 Check if Asset Allocation Is in Line with Financial Goals

Combine and Categorize: The first step in our *Inspection* is to identify and put all the financial and investment assets into one big bucket: his and her IRAs, joint accounts, 401ks, investment property, CDs, and money market accounts. This analysis *breaks the shell* of each mutual fund, unit investment trust, exchange-traded fund, and variable annuity subaccount so we can actually see what's inside them. Then we will categorize each individual holding:

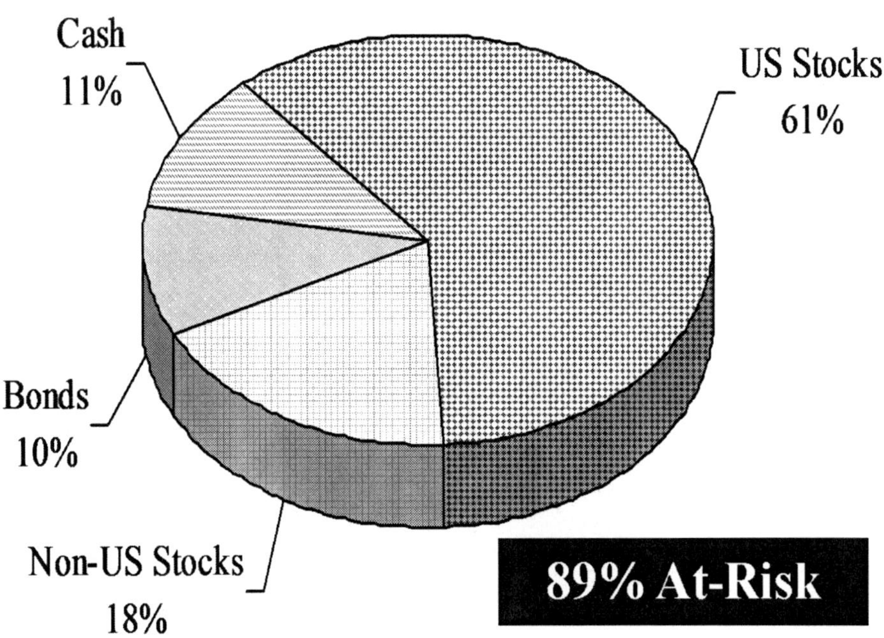

Observations and Assessment: Now, there's no guess work. With this one simple pie chart, we can see exactly how this couple's financial assets are allocated. How much is in stocks, bonds, cash, and annuities? It is easy to see that this couple has 89% of their money at risk (remember, stocks and bonds are both "at-risk" securities). The big, obvious question is, "Is this appropriate?" Taking into account the couple's age, personal situation, years until retirement, income needs, and tolerance for risk, this allocation can now be judged as appropriate or not. For many of those who are already retired, this allocation would be way too aggressive. Make sure you understand and are comfortable with your allocation.

#2 Determine Whether There Is Adequate Stock Diversification

Measure and Monitor: The second step in our *Inspection* looks closely at whether or not we are keeping our stocks diversified enough. Stocks (also commonly referred to as equity securities or equities) play a significant role in financial planning and money management, both before and after retirement. Before retirement, equities are commonly used to accumulate assets for retirement. After retirement, equities can help to hedge against inflation and asset depletion. However, equities also carry substantial risk.

Overall risk can be reduced (but not eliminated) by monitoring and managing a portfolio's diversification. There are three primary ways that an equity portfolio's diversification can be viewed and evaluated: investment style, sector exposure, and global allocation.

Current Account Equity Style

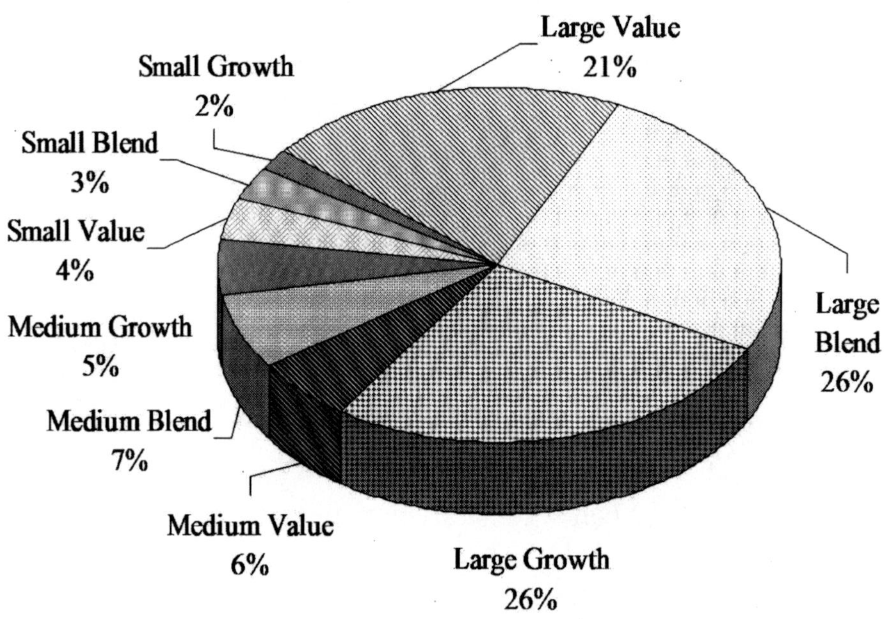

A portfolio with good diversification will have money spread across different size companies: large companies, medium-sized companies, and small companies. In addition, a well-diversified portfolio will have growth-oriented companies as well as established, dividend-paying companies (thought to be a bargain).

The second way to view and evaluate a portfolio's diversification is its sector weightings. With a proper analysis of a portfolio's holdings, you can determine how much is invested in each economic sector.

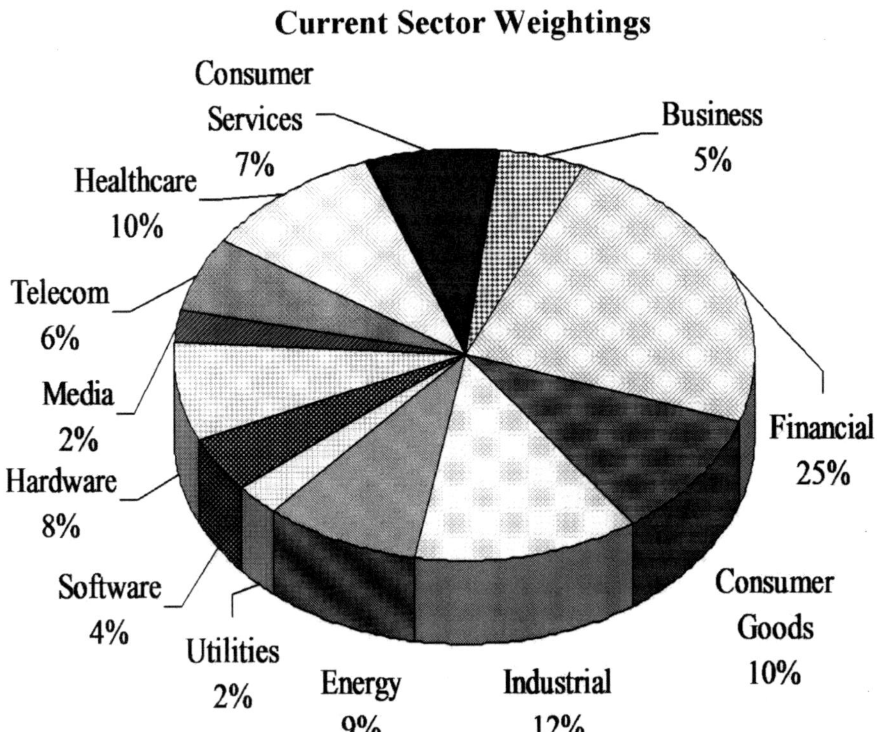

At my advisory firm, we don't usually recommend more than 20 to 25% in any one sector unless we are intentionally putting more into a sector. There can be times when this limit might be exceeded based on an individual's needs.

The third way to judge a portfolio's diversification is to look at where the money is invested around the world. Again, unless we target a particular region on purpose, it is advisable to divvy funds up across several geographic regions. Because of its size, an extra helping of North America (United States and Canada) is also a common approach. Any unplanned concentrations, however, require further analysis to determine the proper course of action.

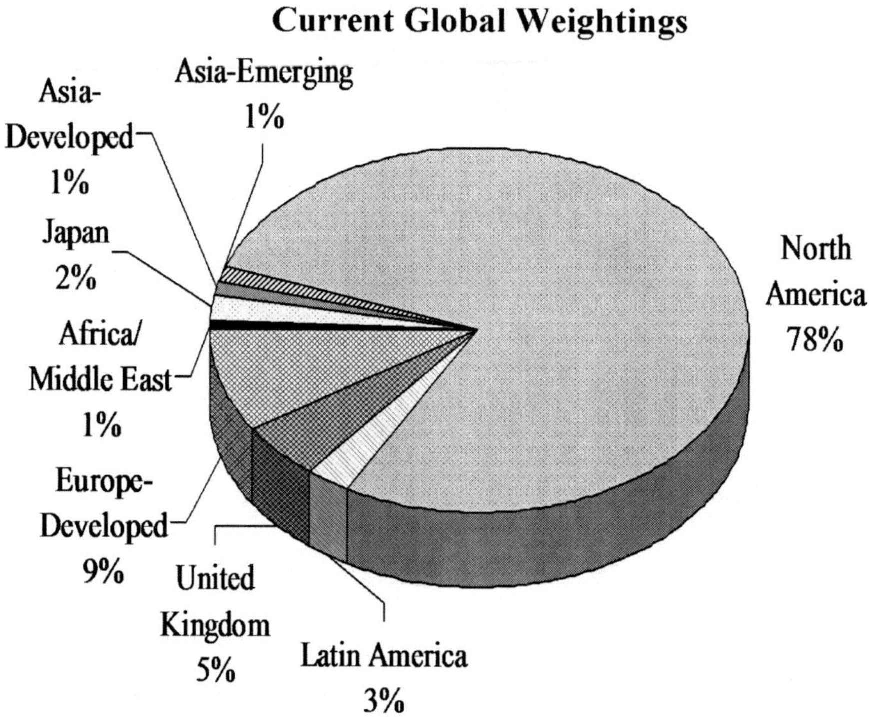

Keeping Them in Line: By avoiding an *out-of-whack* allocation in each of these categories, investors can reduce their chances of having *too much money in the wrong place at the wrong time*. Over time, a portfolio can lose its diversification; some investments do better than others at different times and mutual funds might buy the same types of stock. The key is to monitor and make ongoing adjustments to keep the portfolio in line.

#3 Identify Any Holdings Over 5% of the Portfolio and Assess Risk

Search and Adjust: The third *Inspection* point identifies any holdings that represent more than a 5% position in the total investment portfolio. This is important for achieving adequate diversification and managing risk. In the example below, there are several individual investment holdings that represent more than 5% of the overall portfolio. If too much money is in one individual holding – and that holding were to suffer a major decline – we could have a problem. However, if we've spread our money across several investments, so that none of them represent a large percentage of the overall portfolio, the negative financial impact from any one of them *going down in a ball of flames* is significantly reduced.

Current Investment Holdings

Name	Ticker	Market Value	Portfolio Weight
Cash	-	$825.00	0.70%
Realty Group	RG	$1,426.00	1.21%
MidCap Blend Inst	MBI	$2,958.38	2.52%
Government & High Qual Bd Inst	GH	$3,292.08	2.80%
ABC Funds New Perspective	AFNP	$4,777.11	4.07%
ABC Funds Invmt Co of Amer A	AFIC	$5,667.00	4.83%
Bond Funds	BF	$7,005.39	5.97%
Excel Small Cap Value B	-	$9,253.84	7.88%
Excel Real Estate S	-	$10,072.70	8.58%
ABC Funds Growth Fund of Amer A	AFGF	$11,134.68	9.48%
Excell Cap Apprec S	-	$13,338.35	11.36%
Excel International	-	$14,143.58	12.05%
500 Index Investor	INX	$16,708.27	14.23%
Large Cap S&P 500 Index Inst	LC	$16,804.96	14.31%
	Total	$117,407.32	100.00%

Action Plan: Once we have identified whether there are any individual holdings that represent more than 5% (such as in the box above), we can decide if any holdings need to be pruned back. Other considerations, such as taxes, dividends, or a personal attachment, should be weighed against the risk of concentrating money. Even if the particular holding has performed well in the past, it might be smart to take some gains off the table.

#4 Identify Stock Holdings Over 1% of Portfolio and Assess Risk

Ignorance Isn't Bliss: *The* fourth *Inspection* point identifies any stocks that represent more than a 1% position in the portfolio. It certainly isn't a crime to have more than 1% of a portfolio invested in one stock. The important thing is to make sure that any greater concentrations are on purpose, instead of by accident. Also, if too much money is invested into just a few stocks, overall portfolio risk does increase.

Mutual funds are often the culprit when the percentage invested in one stock goes over 1%. How do you know, for example, if your mutual funds own a lot of the same stocks? A simple way is to use the Morningstar Stock Intersection Report to look at the top stock holdings in a portfolio. By entering in the quantity of each security (stocks and mutual funds) owned, we can figure out which ones represent the largest percentage of the portfolio (as identified in box below). Then we can look for ways to correct the situation.

Top 25 Holdings of Equity Allocation

Stock	Ticker	Percentage of Investments
Group Realty	GR	2.71%
Property Group, Inc.	PGI	2.06%
XYZ Corporation	XYZ	1.81%
Smith Bank	SB	1.60%
Asia Investment Corporation	AIC	1.25%
Fargo Company	FC	1.03%
Realty LP Shs of Benef Int	RB	0.96%
Software Corporation	SC	0.75%
Business Machines Corp	BMC	0.57%
Mobil Corporation	M	0.52%
Yeng International Inc	YII	0.45%
Goody, Inc.	GOOD	0.40%
Casey Warner, Inc.	CW	0.39%
Mack & Co Inc	MCI	0.37%
Peterson, Inc.	P	0.35%
AGP, Inc.	APG	0.35%
Pficer Inc.	PFC	0.34%
Equity Corp.	EQ	0.33%
Alexandrian Pipeline, Inc.	AP	0.30%
Highland Hotels & Resorts, Inc.	HHR	0.28%
Sam-Smith Company	SS	0.28%
Centas, Inc.	CTR	0.27%
Procter Company	PR	0.27%
NY Properties, Inc.	NYP	0.26%
Long Technologies	LT	0.26%
	Total	18.16%

#5 Check the Morningstar Rating for Each Holding

***Apples-to-Apples* Comparisons:** Morningstar Research has one of the most respected and widely used software subscriptions, and is a popular analytical tool with advisers. It aids advisers in making comparisons and ranking mutual funds and stocks against their peers. This is very helpful when evaluating whether or not a particular mutual fund is generating enough *bang for our buck*. Let's say I am *inspecting* your portfolio and looking at one of your holdings, a small-cap growth fund. Let's assume that fund made 8% last year. Not bad, right? What if I compared your small-cap growth fund against all the other small-cap growth funds and found that the average performance for all funds for the same year was 12%, and the top performing funds did 16%? Now what do you think?

For ease of comparison, Morningstar has developed a user-friendly ranking system. Five stars is the best, while one star is the worst. A mutual fund earning a spot in the top 10% of all funds gets a five-star rating. Likewise, a fund at the bottom of the performance barrel would get a one-star rating. Of course, a Morningstar Rating should not be the only reason to buy or sell a fund, but it does expedite performance comparisons.

Morningstar Rating Definitions

Top 10%: ★★★★★
Next 22.5%: ★★★★
Middle 35%: ★★★
Next 22.5%: ★★
Bottom 10%: ★

This rating provides a measure of a fund's risk-adjusted return, relative to similar funds. Funds are rated from one to five stars, with the best performers receiving five stars and the worst performers receiving a single star.
Risk-adjusted return is calculated by subtracting a risk penalty from each fund's total return after accounting for all loads, sales charges, and redemption fees.

With Knowledge Comes Power and Tough Decisions

Many people are surprised by what they learn during *Inspection* point number five. It can be rather disappointing to learn that you have some lower-rated funds. To find out that you've got a big chunk of your money in poor to mediocre funds can be downright infuriating. The immediate thought many people have is, "then what am I paying for?" Now, if an investor has been picking the funds, I put on a special pair of ballet shoes so I can tip-toe around this subject. You certainly don't want to hear that you've made a poor choice, especially in front of your spouse if you are married. I encourage investors not to take our findings personally, but to stay focused on fixing the problems. The chart below is an example of an investor with 55% of their investment portfolio in lower rated funds.

Current Investment Morningstar Rating

Name	Ticker	Market Value	Portfolio Weight	Morningstar Rating
ABC Funds Invmt Co of Amer A	AFIC	$5,667.00	4.83%	1
Excel Real Estate S	-	$10,072.70	8.58%	2
MidCap Blend Inst	MBI	$2,958.38	2.52%	3
Realty Group	RG	$1,426.00	1.21%	3
ABC Funds Growth Fund of Amer A	AFGF	$11,134.68	9.48%	3
500 Index Investor	INX	$16,708.27	14.23%	3
Large Cap S&P 500 Index Inst	LC	$16,804.96	14.31%	3
Government & High Qual Bd Inst	GH	$3,292.08	2.80%	4
ABC Funds New Perspective	AFNP	$4,777.11	4.07%	4
Excel Small Cap Value B	-	$9,253.84	7.88%	4
Excel Cap Apprec S	-	$13,338.35	11.36%	4
Excel International	-	$14,143.58	12.05%	4
Bond Funds	BF	$7,005.39	5.97%	5
Cash	-	$825.00	0.70%	-
	Total	$117,407.32	100.00%	

If dealing with this bad news isn't emotional enough, an even more difficult discussion occurs when someone has been working with an adviser or broker. A few three-star funds isn't a big problem, but a portfolio that is loaded with ones, twos, and threes . . . that's another story. The harsh reality is that sometimes the adviser is simply *asleep at the wheel* and doesn't monitor fund performance. If a broker sells you a fund, shouldn't he monitor it? Yes. Most investment advisers keep a watchful eye on your purchases because that is what you are paying them to do.

#6 Identify Any Holdings with Investment Fees above 1.5% *and* #7 Evaluate Overall Portfolio Fees

Current Investment Holdings Fee Analysis

Name	Ticker	Market Value	Portfolio Weight	Specific Fund Fees	Weighted Fees
ABC Funds Invmt Co of Amer A	AFIC	$5,667.00	4.83%	2.87%	0.14%
Excel Real Estate S	-	$10,072.70	8.58%	2.72%	0.23%
MidCap Blend Inst	MBI	$2,958.38	2.52%	2.68%	0.07%
500 Index Investor	INX	$16,708.27	14.23%	2.46%	0.35%
ABC Funds Growth Fund of Amer A	AFGF	$11,134.68	9.48%	2.46%	0.23%
Excel Cap Apprec S	-	$13,338.35	11.36%	1.85%	0.21%
Excel Small Cap Value B	-	$9,253.84	7.88%	1.78%	0.14%
Excel International	-	$14,143.58	12.05%	1.70%	0.20%
Large Cap S&P 500 Index Inst	LC	$16,804.96	14.31%	0.98%	0.14%
ABC Funds New Perspective	AFNP	$4,777.11	4.07%	0.85%	0.03%
Government & High Qual Bd Inst	GH	$3,292.08	2.80%	0.85%	0.02%
Bond Funds	BF	$7,005.39	5.97%	0.66%	0.04%
Cash	-	$825.00	0.70%	0.00%	0.00%
Realty Group	RG	$1,426.00	1.21%	0.00%	0.00%
	Total	$117,407.32	100.00%		1.82%

The chart above shows the specific fund fees and the overall fees for an investor's portfolio.

Inspection point six identifies any individual holdings with a fee above 1.5%. Fees above 1.5% are considered high. Fees, however, are just one part of the investment equation and may be justified as long as the specific holding's performance warrants the higher fee. The box in the chart above identifies the funds with fees over 1.5%. If the performance of an individual holding does not justify the higher fee, it should be replaced with an equivalent investment with a lower fee.

Inspection point seven evaluates the overall portfolio fees. The average fee for all the investments in the portfolio is circled in the above chart for evaluation. As with individual holdings, the overall (average) portfolio fee should not exceed 1.5%. There are exceptions to the 1.5% fee maximum, but investment performance is the key factor. All other things being equal, reducing fees will improve the bottom line performance.

#8 Assess Fixed Annuity Rates, Riders, and Costs

The next point in our *Inspection* will assess the rates, riders, and costs of any fixed annuities. Each individual product should be evaluated based on its features, benefits, and costs. To be blunt, some products are simply better than others and an objective review is needed to make that determination. This chart from the analysis shows some of the key features and costs that should be reviewed when evaluating an annuity.

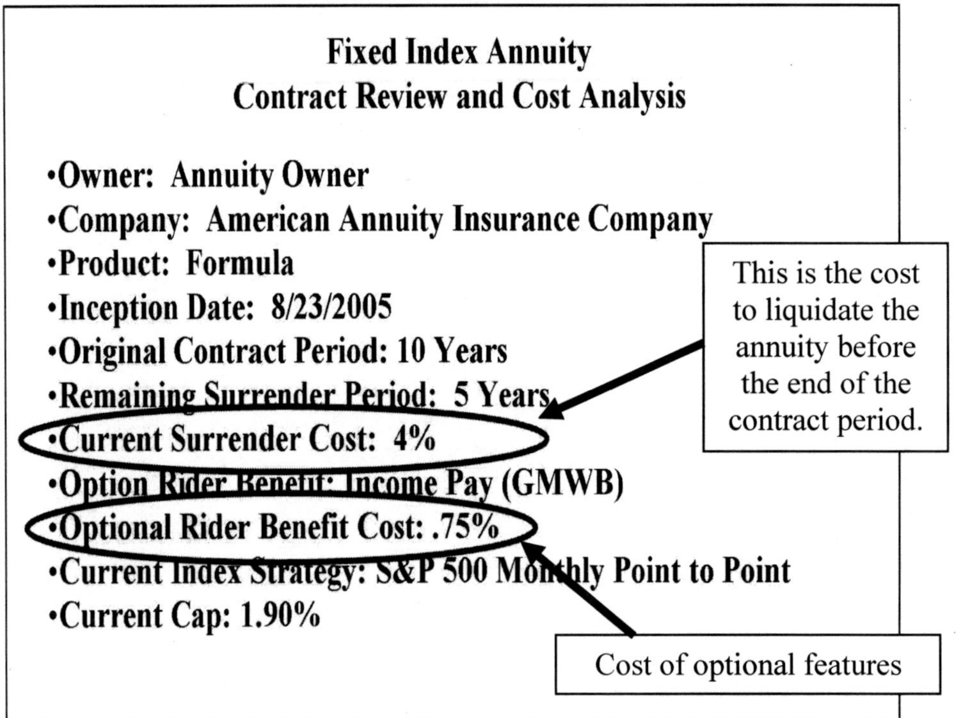

Most insurance companies offer a variety of annuity products, including fixed annuities. Fixed annuities are insurance products that provide safety of principal coupled with interest earnings that will usually be lower than more risky alternatives. The two main types of fixed annuities are: traditional fixed annuities (that earn an interest rate set by the company) and fixed index annuities (that earn a variable rate of interest based on a stock market index).

After a thorough review, advisers can determine whether it is best to keep the annuity, cash it in, or swap it out for a different one. Changing products is only recommended, however, if the cost of contract termination is more than offset by the economic benefits offered by the new product.

#9 Assess Variable Annuity Subaccounts, Riders, and Costs

Inspection point number nine addresses variable annuities. One of the key features of variable annuities is the ability to gain stock market exposure through subaccounts (which are very similar to mutual funds). Unlike fixed annuities, however, variable annuities are securities with the potential for gains and losses. Individual subaccounts are monitored and managed (like their mutual fund cousins) for their star ratings, proper diversification, individual stock exposure, and overall risk. Like any other security holding, a variable annuity should also get an ongoing evaluation; the chart below identifies some of the aspects of that evaluation, including fees. Subaccount fees, mortality and expense charges, administrative charges, and the cost of optional features must all be added together to arrive at the total cost of a variable annuity, which is identified as 3.39% in this example.

Variable Annuity Contract Review and Cost Analysis

Owner: Annuity Owner
Company: Prospective Annuity and Life Insurance
Product: Excel
Inception Date: 3/23/2006
Original Contract Period: 8 Years
~~Remaining Surrender Period~~: 3 Years, 2 Months
Current Surrender Cost: 6.5%

Minimum Guaranteed Income

Subaccounts	Portfolio Percentage	Subaccount Fees	M&E	*Riders	Total	Weighted Fees
Excel Small Cap Value B	19.77%	0.91%	1.55%	0.75%	3.21%	0.63%
Excel Real Estate S	21.52%	1.07%	1.55%	0.75%	3.37%	0.73%
Excel Cap Apprec S	28.50%	1.17%	1.55%	0.75%	3.47%	0.99%
Excel International	30.22%	1.15%	1.55%	0.75%	3.45%	1.04%
Total Average Fee						3.39%

For those approaching or already in retirement, it sometimes makes sense to swap out variable annuities (which are primarily designed for accumulation by taking risks) in exchange for fixed annuities (which are primarily designed for principal protection and lifetime income).

#10 Assess the Quality of Individual Fixed-Income Holdings

If you are nearing or already in retirement, fixed-income holdings may play a bigger part of your financial plan than when you were younger. Safety and consistency of income will take on more importance. The diversification and quality of your fixed-income investments may determine how well you sleep at night!

Point 10 of our *Inspection* examines the quality of individual fixed income, such as bonds, held inside mutual funds. Morningstar has given advisers the ability to evaluate the credit quality of mutual funds by providing the S&P credit ratings for the fixed-income holdings inside each mutual fund (the lowest rating is D and the highest is AAA). Below is an example of a portfolio comprised of bonds of varying quality. The selection of lower versus higher quality bonds will depend on the goals of the investor. Generally, higher quality bonds pay less interest, but have less risk of default, while lower quality bonds pay more interest, but carry more risk. Depending on the individual investor's income needs and tolerance for risk, the portfolio can be adjusted for more income versus more safety.

Current Mutual Fund Fixed-Income Portfolio Credit Rating

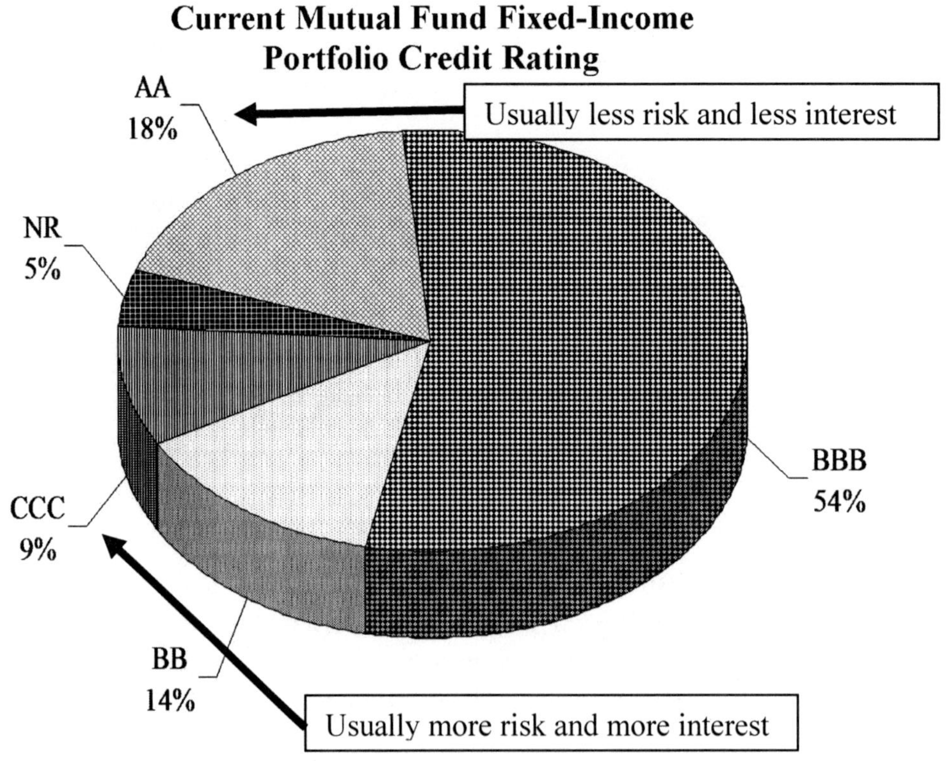

#11 Determine if There Is Adequate Bond Diversification

Next we can investigate the diversification of the current bond portfolio with *Inspection* point 11. Using our Morningstar-enabled microscope, we can peer inside the mutual funds to see the types of bonds, their credit quality, and the length of maturity. Once we understand the composition of a bond portfolio, we can make adjustments to strike a proper balance between risk, interest-earning potential, and prudent diversification. All other things being equal, longer term bonds can earn more interest than shorter term bonds. However, longer term bonds are more susceptible to interest rate fluctuations (that means they can be more risky). So, when we combine the maturity of bonds and their credit quality at the same time, parts of the bond portfolio could be much more risky and volatile than other parts. For example, a lower quality/longer term bond is going to have much more earning potential, and substantially more risk, than a higher quality/shorter term bond. The portfolio in this example is comprised of short and intermediate bonds that vary in quality. Depending on the investor's goals and whether interest rates are going up or down, this portfolio might be just right, or it might need adjustments.

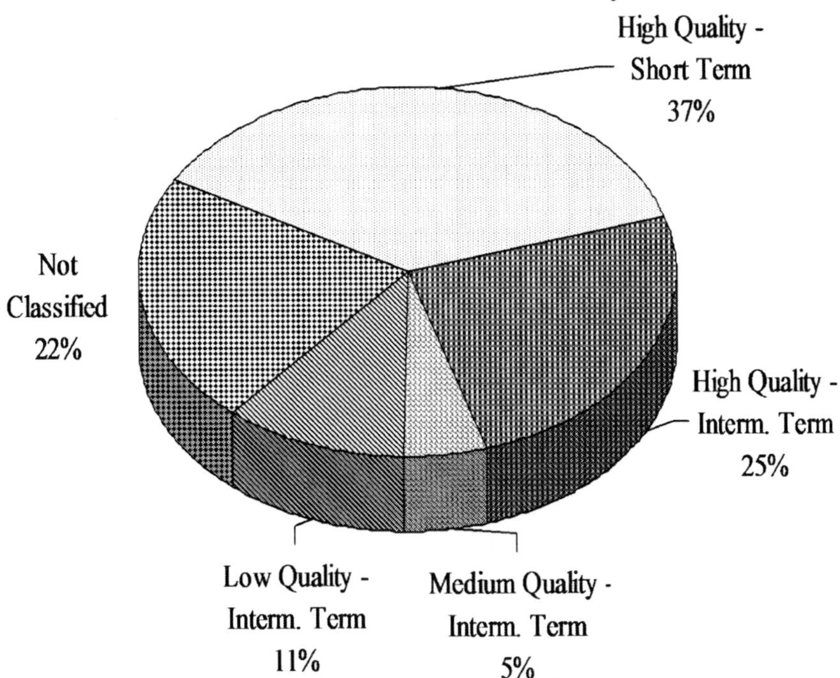

#12 Identify Bond Maturity and Assess Interest Rate Risk

Many advisers make bonds part of their investment portfolios. As retirement approaches (or unfolds, for those already there), bonds often become a larger part of an investment portfolio in order to dampen portfolio volatility and stock risks. U.S. Treasuries are considered by many as the highest quality of bonds (least risk) and consequently, have the lowest yield. The lowest quality bonds (riskiest) are called junk bonds, and they usually have the highest potential yield (they are also politely referred to as "high-yield bonds").

Point 12 of the *19-Point Investment Inspection* examines mutual fund bond holdings to determine their average maturity and average credit quality. Here's an excerpt of this analysis that reveals the overall credit quality and the average length of maturity for an investor's bond portfolio.

Current Mutual Fund Fixed-Income Portfolio Summary

- Average Maturity: 6.29 Years
- Average Credit Quality: BBB

Bonds are sensitive to interest rates. Since a bond's value will usually decline when interest rates go up and increase when interest rates go down, it is important to monitor the current and expected direction of interest rates. The length of bond maturity takes on greater importance when interest rate changes appear imminent. For example, if interest rates are expected to rise, we should be careful not to have too much of the bond portfolio invested in longer-term bonds.

In order to minimize interest rate risk, the maturity dates of bonds should be staggered so that they don't all mature at one time. This allows the investor to take advantage of better bond offerings that may come in the future or to move money into other investments if rising interest rates will negatively impact bond holdings.

#13 Evaluate Current Bond Yield Versus Maturity and Credit Ratings

Point 13 identifies the current income, current yield, average maturity, current market value, and credit ratings of any individual bonds held in a portfolio (data provided by Fidelity BondTrader Pro). Standard & Poors developed a credit rating system for bonds that ranges from D (Bankrupt or in Default) to AAA (Highest Quality). Both parts of this inspection point are helpful in evaluating the performance and the risk of an individual bond portfolio. As can be seen below, there are many points to consider when properly evaluating a bond portfolio for risk, return potential, and appropriateness for an individual investor.

- Maturity Value: $77,000.00
- Market Value: $53,752.24
- Current Year Income: $ 3,936.50
- Average Coupon: 5.248%
- Average Current Yield: 5.517%
- Average Maturity: 4.45 Years

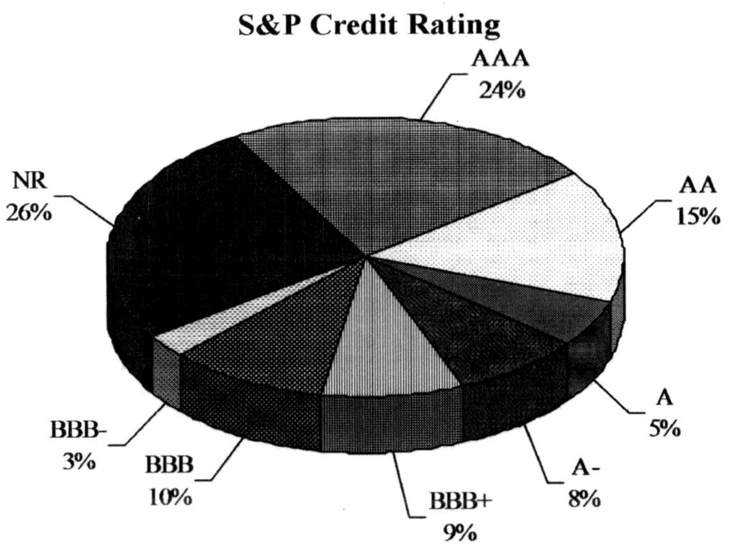

#14 Review Plan for Long-Term Care

With life expectancy on the rise, long-term care has become a significant concern for most retirees. Approximately 70% of people over 65 years of age will need long-term care at some point during their "golden years." In most cases, long-term care starts in the home, can move on to an assisted living facility, and possibly end in a nursing home. Regardless of where long-term care is delivered, the expenses can be substantial. Surprisingly, many people ignore or put off the issue, instead of addressing it head-on. Long-term care should be part of an overall financial plan, because the costs of pre-planning *now* can be much less painful than writing checks to a long-term care facility *later*.

Point 14 of the *Inspection* looks at how the costs associated with long-term care will be addressed. Long-term care policies need to be evaluated for the total benefit limit, benefit amount paid, duration of policy benefits, and insurance company financial strength. This chart shows some of those key features that should be reviewed.

Long-Term Care
Contract Review and Cost Analysis

- **Owner:** Policy Owner
- **Company:** Superior Insurance Group
- **Product:** Long-Term Care
- **Total Benefit Limit:** $175,000
- **Monthly Benefit Amount:** $2,917
- **Benefit Duration:** 5 Years
- **Annual Premium:** $1,176

The policy in this example provides long-term care benefits for five years.

#15 Evaluate Overall Strategy for Lifestyle Funding

"How much do I need to accumulate to retire?" For those approaching retirement, this is one of the most important and most debated questions in personal finance. For those already retired, the question becomes, "How do I make sure that I don't run out of money?" *Inspection* point 15 provides a candid assessment of how a desired lifestyle can be maintained throughout retirement. Common questions include the following:

Pre-Retirement Questions	**In-Retirement Questions**
How much money will I need?	How long will my money last?
How and when do I pay off debt?	Can I avoid *dollar-cost-ravaging*?
When can I retire?	How much life insurance do I need?
When should I start Social Security?	How do I address long-term care?
Which pension option is for me?	How can I reduce portfolio risk?
Where do I get extra income?	How do I guard against inflation?

In the example below, a retired couple can know what their retirement income will look like each year starting at age 67 under both desirable and less-than-desirable investment return assumptions.

Comparison of Retirement Income For Joint Lifestyle

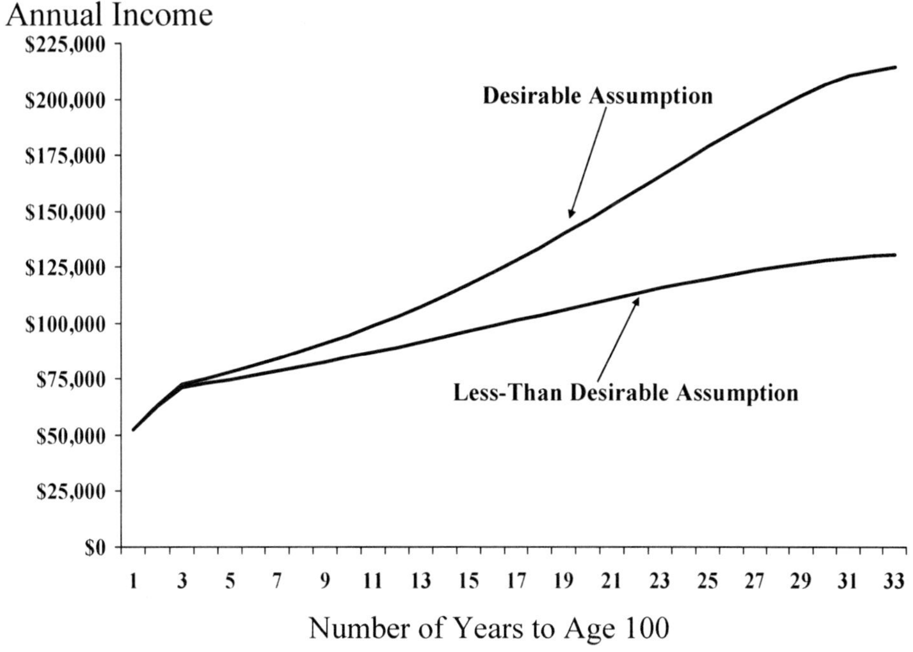

#16 Evaluate Overall Strategy with Survivorship Scenario

Inspection point 16 "pulls the fire alarm" to see what the retirement income and overall financial situation looks like for a surviving spouse. Are there adequate assets to make up for any lost social security or pension income? Will the money last to age 100? Will the money last under less-than-desirable stock market and economic conditions? Is there adequate life insurance to fill any gaps? Are there any adjustments that need to be made now to ensure that the survivor's needs will be met later?

Comparison of Retirement Income for Survivorship Scenario

Less-Than Desirable Assumption

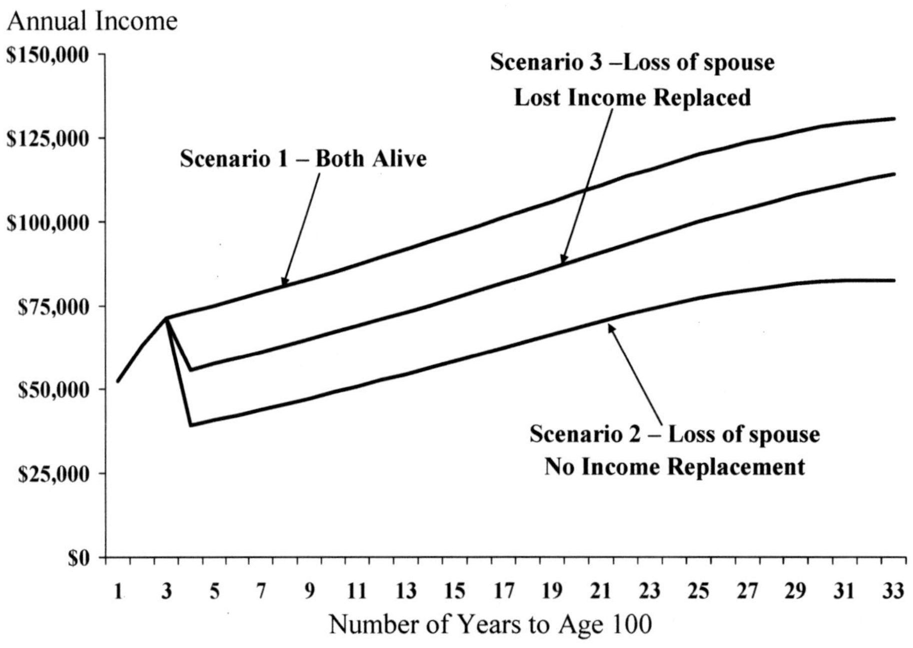

The above chart makes it very clear how a surviving spouse's income can change after the death of a spouse. With this clear information available in advance, a couple can work together (and with their adviser) to develop a survivor income plan. Financial decisions that might otherwise be daunting or confusing during a time of grief can be calmly and carefully addressed. Consequently, a surviving spouse can be left in a much better position if this retirement reality is addressed ahead of time.

#17 Is Life Insurance Adequate or Excessive

As retirees move into retirement, it is not unusual for the need for life insurance to drop or disappear completely. If the house is paid for, if the kids are grown and making it on their own, and if there are sufficient assets to handle joint and survivor income needs, then there may be no need for life insurance. Fortunately, obsolete life insurance can be cashed in, converted to retirement income, given to charity, or simply allowed to lapse. Each person's situation will determine the best approach.

For other retirees and those approaching retirement, life insurance remains an essential financial resource. Many retirees carry a mortgage into retirement. For others, there will be insufficient assets and income at the loss of one spouse. The need for life insurance may be permanent, and the coverage amount may even need to be increased. If that is the case, it is absolutely critical that any existing life insurance policies be reviewed.

The purpose of *Inspection* point 17 is to determine the adequacy of life insurance, whether you even need it, and if you have the best type for your situation. If life insurance is needed, *Inspection* point 17 also examines whether the policy will last and if the insurance company is strong enough to be around to pay future claims. This analysis starts with the chart included below.

Life Insurance Contract Review and Cost Analysis

•Policy Owner:	**Owner**
•Insured:	**Insured Person**
•Company:	**Alpha Life Insurance Company**
•Product:	**Universal Life**
•Inception Date:	**8/1/2000**
•Death Benefit:	**$250,000**
•Current Cash Value:	**$3,779**
•Current Surrender Value:	**$1,500**
•Annual Premium:	**$1,700**
•Beneficiary:	**Spouse**

#18 Assess Portfolio's Overall Risk of *Dollar-Cost-Ravaging*

Are you *robbing Peter to pay Paul*? Are you taking money each month from your investment accounts to meet your current income needs, only to be hurting yourself down the road? *Inspection* point 18 investigates this common "crime." <u>How and where you draw your retirement income is just as important as how much you accumulate for retirement</u>. A few mistakes in planning your distributions can crush your nest egg.

If Social Security and any pensions are not enough to meet your monthly income needs, a consistent source of supplemental income needs to be found. As discussed previously, *dollar-cost-ravaging* can occur when income is withdrawn from brokerage accounts that fluctuate in value. Dividends and interest can be withdrawn without a problem, but liquidating mutual funds, stocks, or bonds in order to meet monthly income needs is how retirement assets get *ravaged.* If you experience investment losses in order to get the cash you need, that's a bad plan. Systematic liquidations from these "at-risk" investments will only work under the most ideal stock market conditions. History has taught us that the stars rarely align in such a cooperative fashion.

Inspection point 18 assesses how sensitive our retirement income plan is to the effects of *dollar-cost-ravaging*, so we can then develop a better approach. In the following hypothetical example, a retiree is cashing in part of her investment portfolio each month in order to meet her living expenses. Sustainable lifetime income could be at risk.

Total Monthly Income Needed	$3,000

Social Security	$ 900
Pension	300
Interest and Dividend Income	300
Investment Portfolio Liquidations	1,500
Total Monthly Income Provided	$3,000

There are a variety of ways to get reliable, supplemental income and avoid *dollar-cost-ravaging*: laddered CDs, laddered bonds, fixed annuities, rental real estate, publicly-traded REITs, and preferred stock. Of course, the best choice will depend on each person's individual situation.

#19 Assess Benefit of IRA to Roth IRA Conversion

Our last *Inspection* point explores the possible benefits of converting an existing Individual Retirement Account (IRA) to a Roth IRA. Despite the complexities that include fees, penalties, tax implications, and predictions about the future, the conversion of an existing IRA to a Roth IRA can be boiled down to one simple question: *When do you want to pay the piper*? In other words, when do you want to pay taxes on your IRA?

Before we examine whether it makes sense to convert an IRA to a Roth IRA, let's begin by understanding the origin of IRAs. IRAs usually get created in one of two ways:

1. In order to shield some of your income from taxes, you elect to open an IRA at tax time. The contribution you make to the IRA comes right off the income you report on your 1040. Smart move!

2. You and your employer make contributions to your retirement account. Then, when you are ready to retire or you leave the job, you roll your 401(k), 403(b), 457, pension cash value, or other employer-based qualified account over into a self-directed IRA.

Regardless of how it got there, in most cases the entire value of what's in the IRA has never been taxed. You may be wondering why the United States Treasury Department and their collection arm – the Internal Revenue Service (IRS) – would give you the ability to put off taxes until later. There are two primary reasons for the favorable tax treatment of IRAs.

Tax Break Reason #1: By letting you skip income taxes on the money you put into an IRA or a retirement account at work, the government becomes your business partner! They hope your account grows handsomely over your working years, so when you do start to draw on it, it will be a much larger account. Because you didn't pay taxes on what you put in it, every last dollar in the IRA will be subject to income taxes when you start to take it out (some IRA holders also have to pay state and city taxes on that income as well). The IRS will require mandatory draws from your IRA when you turn 70½.

Tax Break Reason #2: While some people might want to see America turn into a "Nanny State," where hard-working taxpayers foot the entire bill for everyone else, our current system focuses on helping American workers to save for their *own* retirement. Our government is simply incenting the behavior they want from us. They ring the *tax bell*, and we come a runnin' like *Pavlov's Dog*. As with many financial decisions, there are advantages and disadvantages of converting a Traditional IRA to a Roth IRA. Each person's individual situation and their expectations about the future should be carefully considered.

Roth Conversion Advantages	Roth Conversion Disadvantages
Taxes can be paid in full on the entire IRA at current, known tax rates. This can be a significant advantage since no one knows how high tax rates might go in the future. Unless Congress changes the rules, future tax hikes won't apply to Roth IRA income since you've already paid the tax. Once converted, all future growth in a Roth IRA will not be taxed as income. Required Minimum Distributions (RMDs) are no longer required once a Traditional IRA is converted to a Roth IRA.	Conversion tax (that's the extra tax we pay from converting all or part of an IRA to a Roth IRA). This income generated from converting gets added on top of all the other sources of income, so it could be exposed to a higher tax bracket. This conversion income can also cause more taxation on Social Security and trigger the phase-out of personal exemptions and deductions. Since tax law changes are hard to predict, future tax rules may not be as friendly to Roth IRAs.
At the owner's death, a Roth IRA beneficiary can roll it into his or her own name: there are no income taxes due on that rollover, and there are no income taxes due when the beneficiary draws from the Roth.	Converting an IRA to a Roth IRA before you turn 59½ can trigger a 10% income tax penalty on the amount converted if you do not observe certain distribution rules.
Retirement income drawn five years after an IRA is converted to a Roth IRA isn't taxable and doesn't get counted toward the income limits that determine how much of your Social Security gets taxed.	Income tax brackets may not be higher in future years, so the Roth IRA conversion may have resulted in higher taxes than if you had simply kept it as a Traditional IRA.

Secret #8: How to Build a Retirement Income Plan

You'd probably expect it to be difficult for me to give you a one-sentence explanation of why you should bother with retirement income planning. Given the complexity of the subject and my tendency toward over articulation, I would understand any skepticism. Actually, this will surprise you: I can give you ***all the reasons*** you need to build a retirement income plan with just two words:

Financial Independence

Everything covered in this book is about helping you achieve personal financial independence. That *is* the secret to a secure retirement.

Cheap, but well-run mutual funds are a step in the right direction. Not giving money to your kids that you might need yourself is wise. Planning ahead for long-term care is another smart move. Fighting inflation, getting better interest on your money, reducing portfolio risk through diversification, avoiding *dollar-cost-ravaging*, and putting some of your money in a safe place, these are all essential parts of building a plan to achieve your own version of financial independence. While each of us may have a different expectation for our "golden years" and the legacy we want to create for our heirs, most of us would agree on the three goals that must be met for retirement security to become a reality:

1. Avoid the threats that can drain finances and crush dreams
2. Get what you need from your financial assets during your lifetime
3. Leave the left-over assets to your heirs and beneficiaries

This chapter will focus on how we (you) can achieve these three essential goals. We need to cover a few basics and a little financial planning philosophy. Then, I'll share an example of real life retirement planning. Here's some very good news: if you find an adviser who you like, who really knows what he or she is doing, and who can help you successfully address and implement what we cover in this book, you will be well on your way to declaring your own personal Financial Independence Day. Now let's talk about the planning you need to do to get there.

Two-Glasses-of-Wine-and-the-Back-of-a-Napkin-Planning

Sound financial planning takes more than a few scribbles on a cocktail napkin before dinner. How do you achieve your financial goals and avoid the threats to your retirement security? Based on the hundreds of plans I've built for my clients over the years, I believe true financial independence can be achieved with just three steps. I do not want to over-simplify, but too often retirement income planning seems impossibly complex. When you boil it all down, I am completely convinced that you really can reach your retirement goals if you exercise self-discipline, hire a *great* adviser, and build a financial plan.

In this section, I will help you understand how to overcome the common retirement threats, the process of working with an adviser, and what retirement income planning looks like.

Tell Me More about Those Three Steps to Retirement Security

Please do not take my attempt at retirement planning simplification as "do these three things, and your life will be wonderful!" Blanket assurances are only supposed to be made at 2AM on infomercials. My goal is to break down this big, ambiguous process into more manageable pieces.

Let's address the hardest one first: it is about *you*. No financial adviser is savvy enough to make up for a client who has no self-discipline or control. There are no *magical* financial strategies to replenish an investment portfolio that has been exhausted by an over-indulgent parent. The same is true for people who cannot rein in their own personal spending, before or after they retire. Taking frequent and large withdrawals from your investment account is impossible to support. Although it may sound like a cliché, personal financial independence starts and ends with each person. Financial success is not *one big crap shoot* or purely *the luck of the draw* as some might suggest. If we focus on our retirement security and take responsibility for the outcome of our own financial decisions, we can make real progress.

> *Exercise Self-Discipline to Stop:*
> - ✓ *Dangerous Family Support*
> - ✓ *Excessive Withdrawals*
> - ✓ *Unsustainable Lifestyle*

That brings us to the most important financial choice we need to make: hiring a *great* adviser. Why does the adviser need to be *great*? Just look at the box on the right and the threats an adviser can help you avoid. If you find an adviser who has real credentials, a truck-load of experience, a solid reputation, and the ability to advise you objectively, you will be able to relax. Once hired, it becomes the adviser's job to recommend the right strategies and investment mix to keep your expenses low, help you make smart tax moves, avoid large investment losses, and guard against financial scams.

> *Hire a Great Adviser to Avoid:*
> - ✓ *Wrong Investment Mix*
> - ✓ *Large Losses*
> - ✓ *High Fees*
> - ✓ *Dumb Tax Moves*
> - ✓ *Financial Scams*

Communicate. Relax. Repeat.

Ongoing communication with your adviser is good for both of you, especially at the beginning of the relationship when your personalized retirement income plan is being constructed. Your adviser can build a plan that will help you to withstand the serious threats to your retirement security. The reason I say "withstand" is because each of the events listed in this box will either happen or not. For example, if there is another terrorist attack, your portfolio would likely drop in value, but because your adviser arranged for a chunk of your money to be "off-the-table," you would only see a drop in your investment account. Also, because he kept your "at-risk" money well-diversified, your portfolio wouldn't be affected like the overall market. Of course, no amount of planning can miraculously transform low interest rates, high inflation, or a bear market into ideal economic conditions. Yet, a well-built plan <u>can</u> get you through those tough times. Your adviser can also guide you on how to maintain adequate emergency cash reserves and how to efficiently address long-term care costs. With threat defenses in place, your adviser can then focus on what matters the most: you and your family. Every retiree (and *retiree-wanna-be*) I've ever met has told me that they want a steady stream of lifetime income and the occasional lump sums for trips, gifts, and new cars. And when they're finished with the money, most people want their beneficiaries to get the leftovers. Your adviser can create a lifetime income for you that isn't left to chance. With the help of an attorney, an adviser can also create your personalized financial legacy. You can make sure your heirs get your assets how and when you would have wanted (as if you were writing the checks yourself).

> *Build a Plan to Withstand:*
>
> - ✓ *Poor Market Performance*
> - ✓ *Low Interest Rates*
> - ✓ *High Inflation*
> - ✓ *Cash Emergencies*
> - ✓ *Long-term Care*

> *Build a Plan to Provide:*
>
> - ✓ *Lifetime Income*
> - ✓ *Lump Sums*
> - ✓ *Legacy to Heirs*

Putting the Wheels on the Pavement

By now, you know what a retirement income plan and a great adviser are supposed to do for you. So, how does the adviser put the plan together? Different organizations may recommend a variety of steps to planning and working with advisers. Of course, each adviser may also use a different approach. Here are seven steps I've seen commonly used by advisers:

1. **Adviser Employment**: Once you have chosen your adviser, it's time to hire him or her. This may be done with a formal agreement when you work with a fee-based adviser or with a *gentleman's understanding* if the adviser is to be paid a commission to recommend financial products (such as mutual funds, annuities, stocks, and bonds).

2. **Interview and Fact Finding**: Once you've interviewed advisers to make your selection, the responsibility then shifts to the adviser to interview you and understand your situation. It would be difficult (and I think irresponsible) for an adviser to make financial recommendations to you without understanding your situation.

3. **Financial Analysis**: A helpful part of the "understanding" phase for an adviser is to analyze your current investments. The adviser gets a clear picture of what you need from an interview and then compares that assessed need to the investments you already own. This helps the adviser evaluate *what's working* and *what's not*. The *19-Point Inspection* we reviewed in the previous chapter is this type of a financial analysis.

4. **Financial Planning Recommendations**: Next, the adviser makes recommendations to help you achieve your retirement income goals and address the threats to your retirement security. Expect recommendations to be in writing. The back of a napkin is for dreams and inventions, not for a well-built financial plan.

5. **Discussion/Modification of Recommendations**: Advisers need client feedback to better customize their recommendations. If you don't understand something, please speak up. With your input, the

adviser may modify his or her recommendations to better fit your needs. Once you are in agreement, the plan can be implemented.

6. **Implementation**: Once you've decided to move forward with the adviser's recommendations, the real work begins for the adviser. The financial industry is still a *document-driven* business, so you can expect to complete and sign many forms. The adviser will also need your approval and assistance to move monies around.

7. **Ongoing Service and Communication**: Once everything has settled into place and your plan has been completely implemented, please make sure you get copies of all the final documents that were used to establish your plan; if problems pop up down the road, you may need them. Also, make sure you understand how often you will talk and/or meet with your adviser regarding your investments. Can you call anytime with a question? Does the adviser charge extra for face-to-face meetings? How will your plan be administered? What happens if you need to change your plan? Is it carved in stone or jello? Can the plan be revised as your life changes?

Next Stop: the World of Financial Planners

In this section, I've pulled in four key presentation slides from my work with actual clients, so we can *get the car out of the garage* and *out on the track.* We'll focus on just the slides that show the overall retirement income plan. By this point in the planning process, I would have already gained a complete understanding of the client's personal financial goals and income needs through our *19-Point Inspection.*

In addition to the slides shown here, my typical planning presentation will include slides with important details and the appropriate supporting documentation for investment management services and/or any financial products that have been recommended. As you review these slides, please bear in mind that I use them to explain my recommendations and the planning that is needed. No slides like these should ever take the place of financial product brochures, disclosures, or even those boring investment prospectuses. All identifying information has been removed for this example.

The ~~Millionaire~~ $326,000 Couple Next Door

One of the popular television shows during my teenage years was *Hart-to-Hart*. The show aired from 1979 to 1984 and was about a sophisticated millionaire couple who spent most of their time solving crimes. Back then, "millionaires" were rare. Of course, adjusted for 30 years of inflation, that $1 million from 1980 is now only worth about $326,000 in 2010. In 2011, there are probably over a million millionaires just in the United States.

A few years ago, a modest, unassuming couple with just over a million dollars in retirement assets came to me for planning. Of course, you'd never know they had over a million dollars because "John" and "Mary" are regular people living right next door to you and me. They accumulated their substantial retirement nest egg through a lifetime of prudence and hard work, not by winning the lottery or some other form of instant wealth. John and Mary came to me for financial planning in 2009 after they had recouped some of their 2008 investment losses. John and Mary knew they had taken on too much risk and they wanted to protect their money against the next downturn. They were also concerned about inflation. Here are actual slides that we used along with some explanation of their retirement income planning.

How Much Is There to Work With?

	IRA	Non-IRA
John's IRA Account #1	$ 438,172	
John's IRA Account #2	$ 187,123	
Mary's IRA Account	$ 58,710	
Joint Account #1		$ 196,046
Joint Account #2		$ 167,728
Joint Account #3		$ 47,119
Joint Checking Account		$ 21,411
Total	$ 684,005	$ 432,304
Grand Total	$1,116,309	

19-Point Inspection Completed. Tune-Up Recommended.

Based on my discussions with John and Mary and the *19-Point Inspection* findings, I identified where they could make significant improvements. For those investments that weren't doing well or didn't match their financial goals, we researched and selected better alternatives. We created a customized allocation of their assets to help them achieve their specific goals. What you see below incorporates my recommendations and their "keepers."

What Should We Do with It?

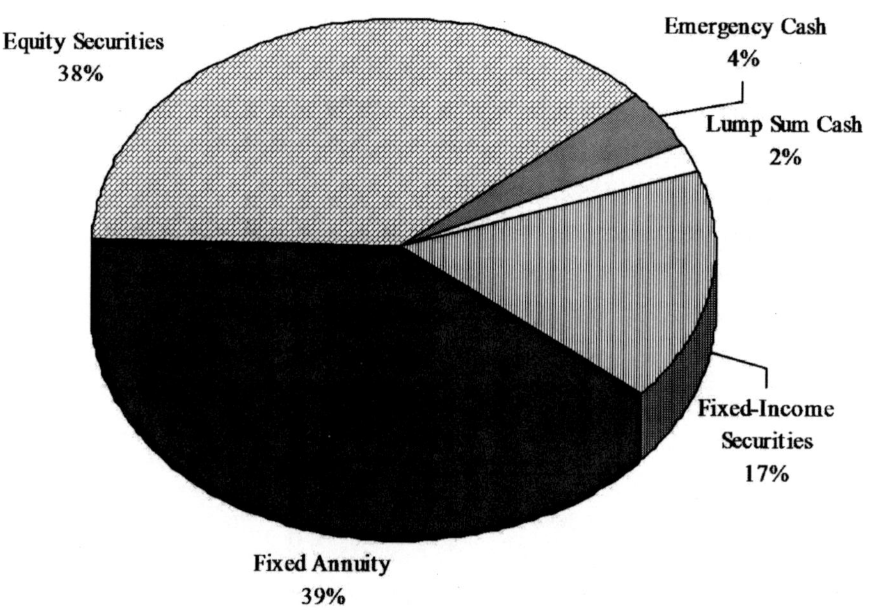

We determined that John and Mary needed to keep about 4% of their assets in a money market account for cash emergencies. Because they also had some upcoming large expenses, we set aside about 2% for cash lump sums. Their next priority was supplementing their pension and social security incomes, so we invested 17% of their assets into a portfolio of fixed-income securities. Based on our expectations about inflation and the need for survivorship income, 38% of their money went to a diversified portfolio of equity securities. To avoid dollar-cost-ravaging and to bring down their overall risk level, the remaining 39% was earmarked for the safe, "not-at-risk" category. For those funds, I chose a fixed annuity.

Where Will My Money Come From?

Two of the biggest retirement concerns people have are "where will my money come from?" and "how long will it last?" With increasing inflation, concerns about social security and company pensions, a volatile stock market, and interest rate changes, these questions have never been more valid. From the work I did for John and Mary, you can see that these questions can be answered with a retirement income plan.

After the initial interview with John and Mary, I understood their current financial situation and sources of income. In the chart below, you can see the sources of their current income: social security benefits and John's pension. To provide them with their desired level of income to age 100, we first created a supplemental source of lifetime income from a fixed annuity (their off-the-table safe money). Second, we built a plan to withdraw money from their investment accounts in a particular order. Each year's income is first drawn from their more stable, conservative investments, and then from their more aggressive funds. This approach reduces the risk of dollar-cost-ravaging. Money invested in the stock market is allowed to do its job (growth and inflation-fighting) for as long as possible.

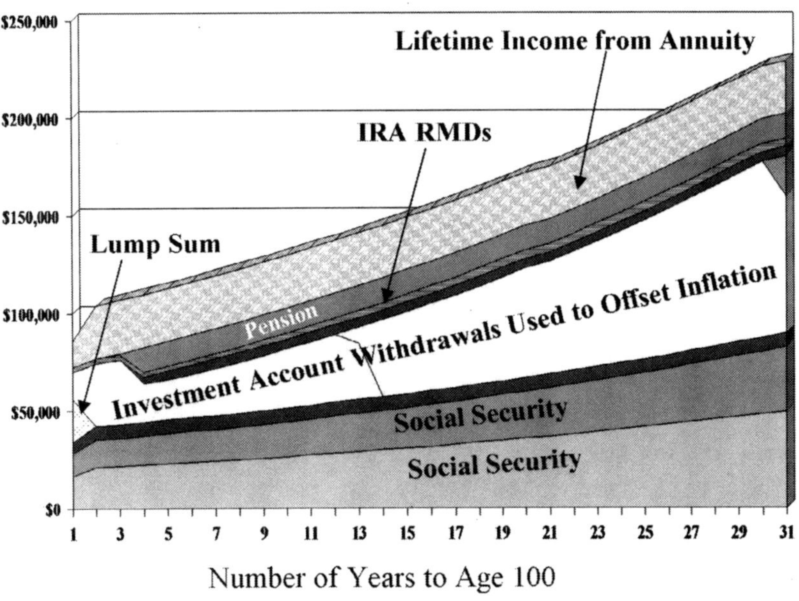

Actual Results Can and Will Vary

With the income projection chart on the previous page, it is easy to see how much of John and Mary's income will come from dependable sources. For the portion of a retirement income plan that actually depends on the performance of equity securities or fixed-income securities, future results will vary according to how good or bad that performance is over time. As a result, it is important to know how much of the total retirement income being generated by the plan is certain and how much is uncertain. Then, we can ask and answer a very important question: how sensitive is the plan to stock market performance?

This next chart helped John and Mary "see" the projected value of their accounts. Should their income needs or personal situation change, it is comforting to know how much all their accounts would be worth and how those values would be affected by future market performance. This chart also provides some insight into how much money might be left over for their heirs.

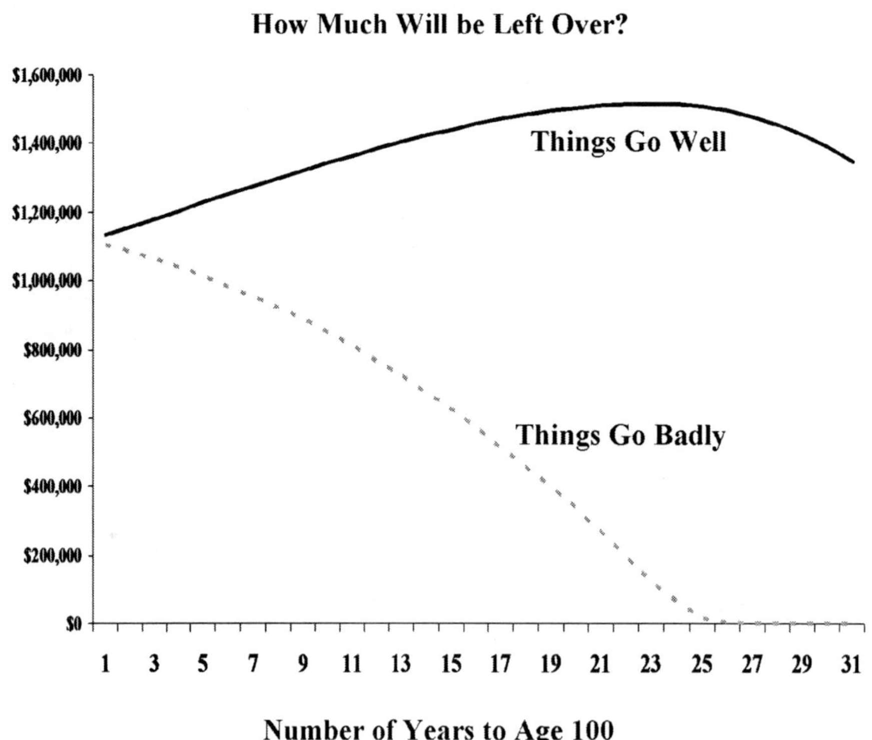

Review of John and Mary's Threat Assessment

Here is a recap of how John and Mary's plan helped them deal with each of the threats to their retirement security:

Threats	**Strategy to Overcome**
Dangerous Family Support	Children are self-sufficient. If needed, financial support is capped at 5% per child.
Excessive Withdrawals and Unsustainable Lifestyle	Withdrawals from the portfolio are capped at what the retirement income plan can support.
Bad Advice	John and Mary took the time to interview and select their adviser based on his experience, education, credentials, and objectivity.
Financial Scams	All financial accounts are held in one of the three *Scam-safe Hideouts*: banks, investment custodians, and insurance companies.
Wrong Investment Mix	Financial assets have been reallocated to provide a balance of safety, income, and growth. Flexibility and control are maintained.
Large Investment Losses	Their "at-risk" money has been reduced to 55% of their total assets. 38% of their money is invested in equity securities and 17% is in fixed-income securities. Both are actively managed and well-diversified.
Poor Market Performance	A large portion of their retirement income is certain. Poor stock market performance affects only the portion of their assets invested to fight inflation. Their plan is built to withstand year-to-year market gyrations.
Dollar-cost-ravaging	Most of their retirement income will come from a pension, social security, and a fixed annuity. Any additional income needed during the first twelve years of their plan will come from lower risk securities.

Threats	Strategy to Overcome
High Investment Fees	No-load mutual funds with low annual expenses and reasonable investment advisory fees have been selected for their portfolios; the fixed annuity has low fees.
Dumb Tax Moves	John and Mary have a CPA prepare their taxes each year. They can contact their adviser to coordinate and discuss financial decisions. Their adviser understands the tax aspects of financial, investment, and retirement planning.
Low Interest Rates	Their fixed-income securities portfolio is well-diversified and represents just 17% of their assets. Their fixed annuity has multiple options to earn interest and a lifetime income guarantee.
High Inflation	38% of their assets are directly invested in the equity market, which has been a very good hedge against inflation.
Cash Emergencies and Lump Sums	Adequate funds have been set aside to address most emergencies that can occur and to provide lump sums of cash when needed.
Long-term Care	John and Mary have purchased long-term care insurance.
Longevity and Lifetime Income	The retirement income plan has been built to provide income through age 100.
Survivorship Income	The retirement income plan has been prepared to provide joint life income and to adapt to the needs of the surviving spouse.
Legacy to Heirs	Based on their plan and how their funds have been invested, there is a high probability that significant funds will be left to John and Mary's children.

How are you dealing with these threats in your financial situation? Planning doesn't have to be hard, complicated, or stressful. It really can be this straightforward! Invest some time today, get your finances in order, and enjoy a financially secure tomorrow.

Section III

Investments as Part of Your Retirement Plan

Secret #9: Commonly Used Investment Strategies

There is no fail-safe strategy that will tell us what the stock market will do on a given day, week, month, or year. This was proven during the market crash of 2008. Some of the largest and most respected financial institutions, who had hired some of the smartest and best paid men and women in the world, went bankrupt! World class companies were caught *flat-footed*. Take a look at what happened from the start of 2008 through the market bottom in March of 2009:

Of course, in the aftermath of a financial upheaval or a raging bull market, we can look back and see which investment strategies worked and which ones didn't. However, advising clients during the stock market meltdowns of 2000 through 2002 and again in 2008 was not easy because when you are in the middle of the storm, predicting stock market behavior is anything but easy.

Despite the obvious challenges of investing, there will always be those who want to tell you about their latest and greatest stock market strategy that will make you millions! They'll happily tell you that if you had used their special strategy, you would have *known* to shift your money out of bonds and stocks in 2008 and into gold for great performance! Uh-huh. Here's a February, 2011 example of an Internet pitch: A self-proclaimed stock market guru says he took his student loan money and made millions of dollars, and now, because he is "bored" with his success, he's offering to teach you his super-secret investing strategies, so you can do the same thing from the comfort of your own home, for the bargain price of $130.

There are hundreds of absurd strategies that come to us in emails, newsletters, financial seminars, radio shows, slanted magazine articles, infomercials, and TV interviews. Fortunately, there are also real investment strategies that are used by professional investment advisers every day. Before we look at these strategies, let's talk about risk.

Risk is a good thing. Risk gets entrepreneurs up at 5AM to start their day. Taking risks creates the opportunity for the long-term growth that we would never see if the investment world were one big mediocre CD. Our economic engines would stall if investors didn't have the opportunity to earn higher rates of return. What would be the point? The heart of capitalism is the opportunity to take risks, to fail, to succeed, and to receive handsome returns in exchange for those uncertainties. In order to accumulate funds for retirement, usually some risk must be taken.

Risk is a bad thing. Risk rouses investors from their sleep to ponder the latest stock market plunge and to debate whether they have more invested than they should. Risk is the possibility that you could lose some or all of the money you put into a security or portfolio of securities. Even in a well-crafted portfolio with a diversified mix of stock, bonds, REITs, preferred stock, and mutual funds, there is risk; it may be reduced, but risk remains. When we invest in equity securities (common stocks, mutual funds, or variable annuities), we are putting our investment principal at risk. The same is true for fixed-income securities (commercial paper, preferred stock, REITs, and bonds). The overall markets have bounced back many times, but individual investments aren't always so resilient, and sometimes they become worthless (e.g., Enron and Lehmann Brothers). That means, literally, we could lose 100% of our money if the investment security goes bad (which is why diversification is so important).

Securities industry propaganda has long encouraged investors to keep all their money invested in the stock market, despite what happens to the market or the economy, or what phase of life someone has reached. And when the markets fall, these risk brokers have two well-rehearsed talking points: "Hey, don't worry; it'll come back," or "Everybody lost money, so you're not alone." This thinking is flawed. The truth is that the market might not come back quickly enough to fix your circumstances (remember *dollar-cost-ravaging*). Also, what other investors experience should give you no consolation, nor should it be relevant to you. If you <u>and</u> one million other people all go bankrupt at the same time, that doesn't make you any less bankrupt. Remember that brokerage firms sell securities (that's what "broker" means) and they want to keep your money *in play* as long as possible. Keep that in mind when they make recommendations.

What Are the "At-Risk" Money Choices?

Done poorly or with too much risk, investing can be a bad thing. Done well and with the right amount of risk for the investor, it can be a great thing! Investors and advisers often choose the following equity and fixed-income securities for their at-risk money:

Should all of our money be put at risk? (That may sound like a loaded question.) Actually, sometimes the answer is "yes." If we are far enough away from retirement, we could invest all of it into securities. Most of the time, however, the answer is "no." Only a portion should be "at risk."

What Are the "Not-at-Risk" Money Choices?

Banks and insurance companies are the primary sources for "not-at-risk" money choices. Banks offer money market accounts and certificates of deposit. Insurance companies offer fixed annuities.

I have long argued (maybe "encouraged" is a better word) that investors should only put a portion of their retirement money into securities. I like to see a good chunk of someone's retirement income come from not-at-risk choices, such as CDs, fixed annuities, and immediate annuities. And, of course, there is always cash, and some people *do* keep it in their safes.

So You Want to Invest? Then I've Got Some Questions.

When we talk about investment strategies and how much risk we will take with our investment portfolio, keep in mind that we're talking about only the money that you have decided to "put at risk." "Not-at-risk" money needs to be *off-the-table* and discussed separately.

Most investment strategies are designed to do two things:

1. Maximize performance for the selected level of risk, and
2. Reduce the risk of loss and volatility for the target performance.

I know this sounds circular, but that's what investment strategies are designed to do: get as much return for the amount of risk taken and minimize the amount of risk for the return desired. Despite the risks that are found in both equity and fixed-income securities, sound investment strategies can achieve these results. You can have your portfolio tailored to the level of risk you are willing to accept. Also, you can have a portfolio that is designed to give you the investment returns you desire. Your money can be managed to generate returns while keeping the risks low.

To guide clients in how much risk they should take with their "at-risk" money, most investment advisers have developed what is commonly referred to as a "risk tolerance questionnaire" or "investment suitability questionnaire." These questionnaires help the adviser and client determine the appropriate level of risk to take with the client's "at-risk" money.

If you choose to hire an adviser to manage your money for you, I cannot over-emphasize the importance of being **honest** when answering the questionnaire. Be candid with the adviser; don't pretend you are more aggressive or more conservative than you really are; don't try to be what you'd like your friends or family to think you are. If you do, you will be very sorry later. Advisers also rely heavily upon the answers you provide on questionnaires to make investment management recommendations. If the adviser has questions or concerns and wants you to complete a more detailed questionnaire, please do it. The better an adviser understands you and your situation, the better his or her advice can be for you.

We Need to Check Your Cholesterol, Lipids, and Risk Tolerance

If your doctor were to ask you to get a second batch of blood work, would you do it? Absolutely! Most people wouldn't return to the doctor's office without getting that blood work done, right? Please give your adviser the same degree of respect, so he or she can do the job well for you.

Once I had a client at my investment advisory firm who flatly refused to complete an extra questionnaire, so we could make sure we had him in the right investment strategy. (Personally, I'd fill out each questionnaire three times with crayons, while hanging upside-down, if I thought it would help the adviser do a better job at managing my account.) There's not much a reputable adviser can or should do, except to say "goodbye," when a client won't provide basic information or clarification about his goals, objectives, financial needs, and tolerance for volatility and loss. A "work with what you got" bravado attitude might be acceptable in other industries or professions, but it simply doesn't work in the business of providing investment and financial advice. Good advisers take these questionnaires, and their assessments of their clients' needs, very seriously. So do the federal and state regulators who are charged with policing advisers and protecting consumers. The forms matter.

These forms also serve to protect you if the adviser does something *out-in-left-field* with your investment account. If you tell your adviser to invest your money conservatively (and your questionnaire agrees with that), then you've got a case against him if you lose a significant amount of money because he invested it too aggressively. Read these questionnaires, including any fine print, carefully. Ask the adviser to define any terms you don't understand. Answer thoughtfully. And, most importantly, if your financial situation changes later, please notify the adviser right away. For example, if you say that you're not going to need any money from the account for five years, and then you find out that you need money to replace your roof, don't wait until the contractor shows up for payment before you tell your adviser. Give your adviser as much notice as possible, so he can determine if your strategy needs to be adjusted. Please also tell your adviser if you are uncomfortable with the amount your portfolio moves up and down. A more stable strategy can be put in place for you, but only if you speak up.

Ever Wonder Why Advisers Are So Obsessed with Allocation?

If we knew which individual investments or sectors of the market would do the best, we wouldn't need to allocate anything; we'd just put all our money into what's going to do the best. Because we can't know that in advance, asset allocation is about spreading our "at-risk" money around. Without a crystal ball, asset allocation helps us to avoid being "all in" at the wrong time in the wrong place. Research has shown that different asset classes (e.g., cash, bonds, stocks, and commodities) can outperform each other during different market cycles and economic conditions.

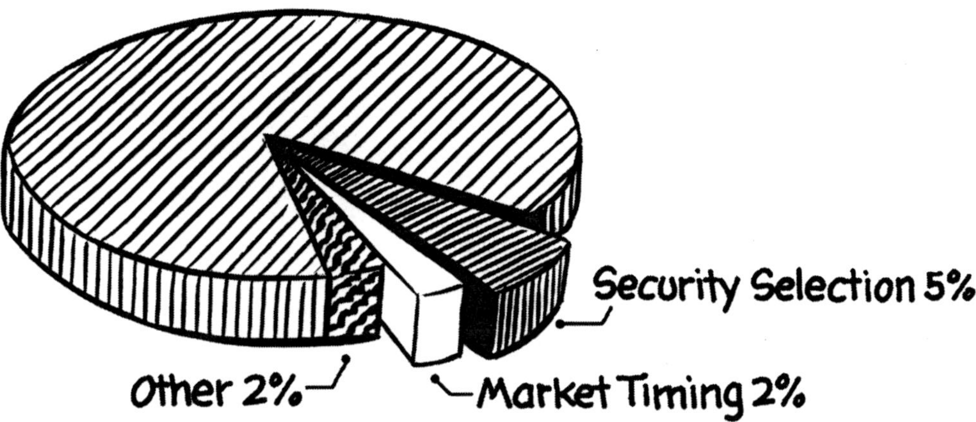

Back in 1986, an important study conducted by Brinson, Hood, and Beebower appeared in the *Financial Analysts Journal.* The study revealed that over 90% of a portfolio's variance can be explained by how it is allocated. Picking the next hot stock or trying to time the market was proven to be less important than getting diversification across different asset classes and investment types. By investing money into unrelated investments like stocks, bonds, precious metals, non-U.S. companies, and real estate, we should get more downside protection than if we just plowed everything into a single stock or one investment category. This is the primary reason why investment professionals spend so much time working on asset allocation and re-balancing their clients' portfolios.

Strategic Asset Allocation: How *Hot* Would You Like It?

Strategic Asset Allocation involves building an investment portfolio with a specific mix of equity and fixed-income securities to get the right "temperature," which is the targeted level of risk. For example, a "growth allocation" might be 85% equity (stocks) and 15% fixed-income (bonds and preferred stocks). Individual securities held in the portfolio might change from time to time with this strategy, but the overall mix percentages are maintained in the face of economic changes and market activity. Here's a simple example of different strategic asset allocations:

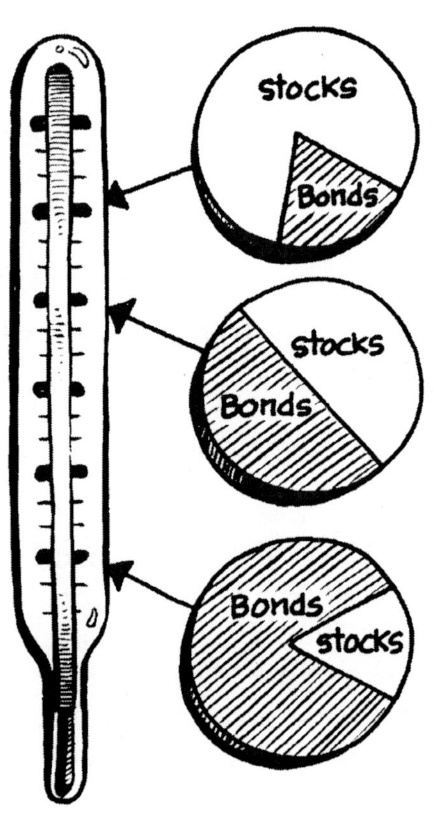

GROWTH

Diversified equity portfolio designed to maximize long-term returns, with fixed-income securities to help temper short-term volatility.

BALANCED

A moderate risk portfolio with an equal mix of equity and fixed-income securities for both capital appreciation and current income.

CONSERVATIVE

Primary emphasis is placed on short-term liquidity. Current income and growth are second and third.

Signs, Portends, and an Asset Allocation to Match

Active Asset Allocation, which is also called "Tactical" or "Trend Following," is similar to strategic asset allocation except that the mix of securities will change based on the adviser's expectations about the economy, financial trends, or shocks to our financial system (such as a terrorist attack). Active asset allocation uses a shorter timeframe of a few months, rather than the multi-year time frames used by strategic asset allocation and the classic *buy-and-hold* strategy. The asset allocation mix might start at 85% equity and 15% fixed income, but then later go to 50% stocks and 50% bonds. This strategy involves a higher level of turnover and more adviser judgment. (Please note that this is not the same as market timing, which is buying and selling securities based upon the adviser's short-term expectations about the direction of the financial markets. I'll get to that shortly). Here's an example of what an active allocation might look like under different *expected* economic conditions:

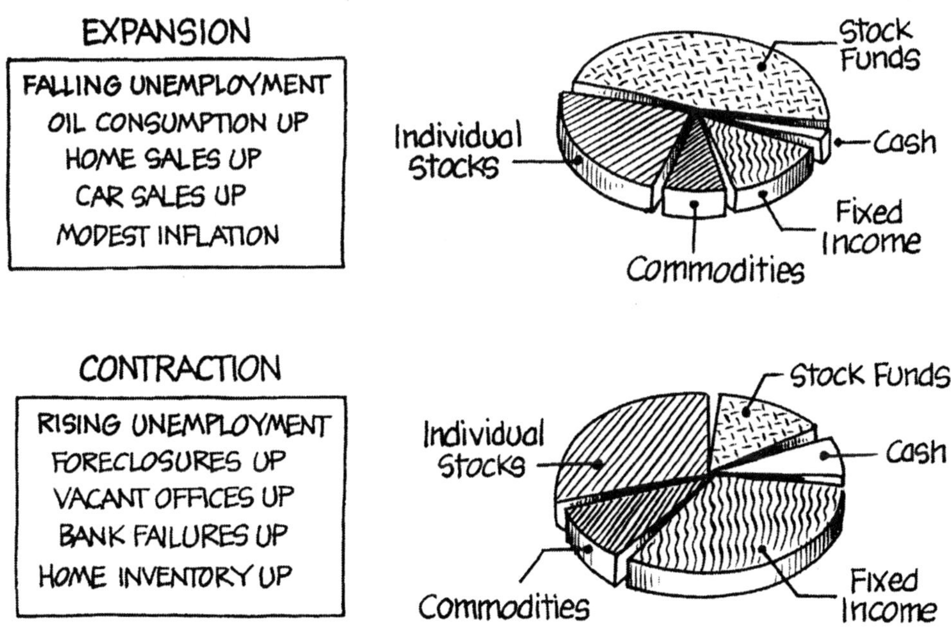

During a period of expansion, a larger percentage of the portfolio would be allocated to stocks. Conversely, a smaller percentage would be allocated to stocks during a contraction.

Buy-and-Hold: Long Hauling Ain't Just for Truckers

We've all heard or received emails declaring that "buy-and-hold is dead!" Absolute statements can be funny or even ridiculous, and this one is no exception. You may remember the famous 1979 *Business Week* headline, "The Death of Equities." Immediately afterwards, as if with a vengeance, the S&P 500 index climbed almost 400% before the popping of the technology bubble in 2000.

During the recent recession, some TV talking heads dismissed the traditional buy-and-hold strategy as ineffective or inadequate. This well-known and often used strategy promotes the idea of buying and holding solid companies or mutual funds for the long haul to get long-term growth. To be rewarded, discipline must be maintained to *keep-on-truckin'* through the market's ups <u>and</u> downs. Of course, the expectation has to be that the long-term outlook is good for the economy and the stock market, for this strategy to make logical sense and financial *cents*.

At the end of 1998, the S&P 500 index was at 1229. By the end of 2010, it closed at 1258. That means the index was up less than 3% total for the entire twelve years. However, during this time, the market had experienced a rally of 68%, a sell-off of 50%, then a 100% advance, a drop of 58%, and then a surge of 83%. These gyrations created opportunities for some investors, but many lost money trying to time the market; they would have done better by staying invested. They should've kept their eyes on the road, hands on the wheel, and foot on the gas!

Three Essential Ingredients for the Buy-and-Hold Recipe

Simply put, longer holding periods have paid off. From 1934 to 2002, 10-year holding periods delivered a positive investment result 100% of the time. One-year holding periods for the same period generated a loss three out of every ten years (Ibbotson Associates, *2003 Yearbook*). Yes, yes, prior performance isn't necessarily indicative of future results, but isn't it interesting that the buy-and-hold strategy still worked for 1999 through 2010 by producing a 2.4% gain during one of our most difficult investing periods? I believe this strategy can work, especially when the markets do better, if we include three essential ingredients:

Seek Professional Investment Advice

Invest Less Than 50% of Your Retirement Money

Get Your Retirement Income Somewhere Else

1. You have to know what to buy and then how long to hold it! Simple enough, right? Actually, that's where the professionals come in, unless stock picking is your hobby. Without competent, objective investment advice, a stock market crash could be financially and emotionally devastating.

2. Don't use the buy-and-hold strategy for all of your retirement money. Why? Most people can't handle seeing their life savings drop 37% (or more) like they did in 2008. Unless your name is *Spock* and you can simply turn off your emotions, I generally recommend that no more than 50% of your retirement money go into this investing strategy.

3. In order for the buy-and-hold strategy to work, you should not require income from your investments. You need to be getting your income from your more conservative accounts or somewhere else.

It's Time in the Market, Not Timing the Market.

I've used charts like the one below for many years to help investors understand the challenges of trying to time the market. Let's review the 2,500 topsy-turvy trading days between 2001 through 2010. Look at what would have happened to an investor's cumulative return if he or she missed just a handful of the better days while trying to time the market:

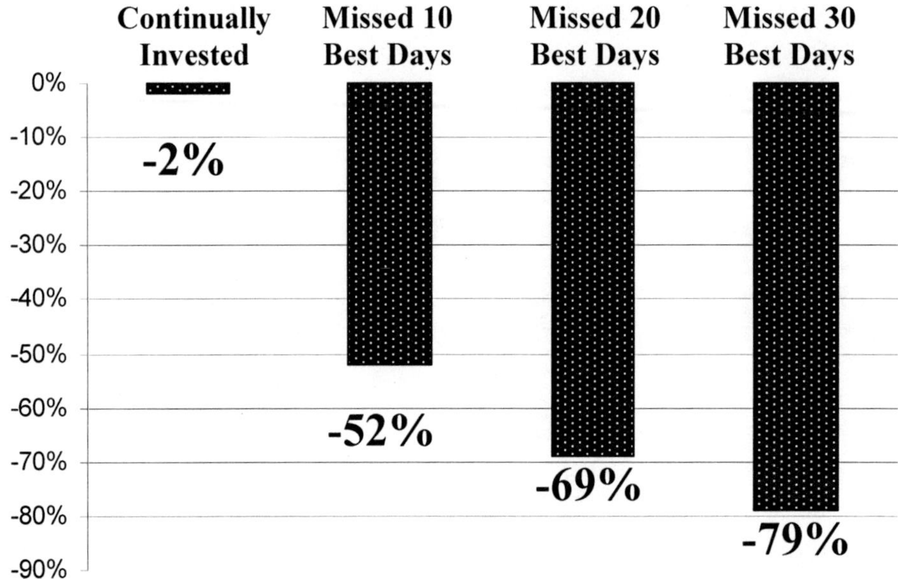

This chart is for illustrative purposes only and is not representative of future performance of any particular portfolio or security. The S&P 500 index is a market-value-weighted index of 500 stocks that are traded on the NYSE, AMEX, and NASDAQ. The Index is a broad-based, unmanaged index and is not available for direct investment. Results shown reflect the reinvestment of dividends, but include no investment fees or consideration of taxation. Past performance is never a guarantee of future results.

Market timing fans argue that all those market swings between 2001 and 2010 created opportunities for savvy investors who knew exactly when to get in and get out. Avoid losses and capture gains? I cannot argue with that. However, I don't know anyone who can consistently "catch the good" and "avoid the bad" days in the stock market. If anyone can tell me what the stock market is going to do next year, or even for just one day, I have a fat salary and a corner office waiting for them. We don't hear much about day traders anymore. Timing the market is very difficult. I'm persuaded that buy-and-hold, asset allocation, and active management are better "at-risk" investment approaches for most investors.

Coming to a Theater Near You: *Investing in 3D*

There is no absolute best way to manage your "at-risk" money. If you hire an investment adviser to manage your money, keep in mind that different advisers will have different opinions on the strategies that should be used. Some advisers believe that the markets are very efficient and that everything that *can* be known, *is* known, and is already reflected in stock prices. As a result, they are going to use a more passive investment strategy. Others believe that profit opportunities exist in changing economic conditions and in picking individual stocks, mutual funds, and exchange-traded funds. This is considered a more active approach.

To recap, most investment strategies used by professional advisers can be broken down into three dimensions:

Dimensions	Passive Approach	Active Approach
Asset Allocation	Strategic Allocation	Tactical Allocation
Investment Duration	Typically a Year or More	Typically a Few Times a Year
Security Selection	Index Funds and Exchange-Traded Funds	Mutual Funds, Exchange-Traded Funds, Individual Stocks, and Individual Bonds

Often, investment advisers will use a combination of the strategies we've discussed. Here are some things to think about when you evaluate investment strategies that might be recommended to you:

- Do you feel comfortable with them, or do they put you on edge?
- Do you agree with the adviser's basic investment philosophy?
- Will the allocation be active or strategic?
- On average, how long will individual investments be held?
- What types of investments will be used?
- How have the strategies performed in the past?
- What should you expect for future returns?

And remember, you can also use multiple strategies for various accounts.

Secret #10: Overview of Investment Securities

We have all seen the videos of the men and women yelling, screaming, and throwing up hand signals. No, I'm not talking about college football games. The chaos-filled environments I'm talking about are the stock exchanges in New York, Chicago, and Philadelphia, where traders buy and sell stocks and scribble down their orders on sheets of paper. This is the heart of what is commonly referred to as the "stock market." Today, of course, not all buying and selling of stocks and other investments is done this way. Each year, more and more investing is done electronically. When one investor or broker inputs the desired stock into the computer, it is automatically matched with someone who wants to sell. No funny jackets are required, unless that's just your thing.

Where Do Stocks Come From?

An obvious question is: where do the stocks come from that are traded on the stock market? "Stock" is created when the owners of a company want more money for their business. They might want to use the money to expand their operations, to refinance debt, or to allow owners to "cash in" on what they've built.

Here's an example: Jim Martin owns Martin Toy Company. He begins selling toys from a local store. Jim decides to franchise his toy stores all over the state of Florida and takes out a loan from a bank to help pay for the new stores. Jim decides that he wants to raise more money to expand his company across the country. He talks to Boldman Slacks, a large investment company who can assist him in turning Martin Toy Company into a publicly-traded stock. Boldman Slacks, for a fee of course, will help Jim send the right paperwork to the Securities and Exchange Commission (SEC), which is the government agency charged with overseeing and regulating all publicly-traded companies.

Let's say that Jim decides that he wants to raise $100 million by selling 80% of his company. The plan is to sell 5 million shares at $20 per share on the open market. Jim plans to keep 20% of the outstanding shares of his company with the idea that 20% of a large, nationwide company will be better than 100% ownership of a small, regional company.

Do I Hear a Bid for $20? How about $25?

When the company "goes public" and starts being sold on the open market to investors, Jim's company will get the $100 million, less various fees paid to accountants, attorneys, and investment bankers. This is called an Initial Public Offering (IPO). The price per share of the company will fluctuate based on how people expect Martin Toy Company will perform in the future. Martin Toy Company, as a publicly-traded company, could potentially end up with thousands of shareholders besides Jim. If Jim remains president of the company, he will report to these investors about how Martin Toy Company performs and grows. If Jim doesn't manage the company well, the other shareholders can fire him.

Hundreds of small and large companies go through this process each year, all in an attempt to raise money, grow, and be profitable. Once they become public, they are required to report their financial records four times per year to the SEC. They must also allow their shareholders, who are the owners of the company, to see how they are performing.

Whenever shareholders want to sell their stock in the company, they simply go into their brokerage account or call a broker. It's an easy transaction for the seller, since most stocks usually have a buyer on the other end wanting to purchase those shares. After the company has had its IPO, the price of the stock is determined by thousands of buyers and sellers in the marketplace. If Martin Toy Company announced that they have tripled sales this year and are reporting record profits, more likely than not, a higher number of investors will want to own Martin Toy Company stock. This increase in number of buyers will act like an auction house. Each investor bids a little more than the last to become an owner of the stock – pushing the price of the stock higher and higher. The same thing can happen in the other direction. If there are more investors who want to sell a stock, they will lower their price in order to find a buyer; it works a lot like trying to sell a house in a down real estate market.

One of the reasons the stock market fell 37% in 2008 was because a lot of investors simply wanted out of the market. People panicked and were willing to take huge losses just to walk away with something. As you can see, supply and demand have a big impact on how individual stocks are "priced" by the stock market and how the overall stock market performs.

Stocks Are Worth Only What Someone Is Willing to Pay for Them.

Stock market "gurus" go on TV each day to tout their latest stock picks: "this one is undervalued and you should buy it to make a profit," or "that one is overvalued and you should get out so you don't lose." What does "undervalued" or "overvalued" mean exactly? Many investors feel the true value of a company can be discovered by reading and researching the company's financial documents and the reports it files with the SEC.

There are different measures that can be used to assess the value and profitability of publicly-traded companies, such as the percentage sales have increased, the amount of debt the company carries, the company's competitive position, or the number of new products the company has released. This, and sometimes a lot more information, is analyzed to come up with what each person thinks is the true "value" of a company's stock. Because of the complexities involved in picking which stocks to buy and sell and at what price, many individual investors look to professional money managers and mutual funds for help. Lots of investors choose not to invest in individual stocks because of the risk involved.

Referring back to our example of Martin Toy Company, let's say we bought stock for $20 a share when the company went public. Now just a few months later, it is worth $24 a share. Once our fictitious Martin Toy Company went public, they issued shares of ownership in the company by offering what is called "common stock." Whenever you hear someone mention "stock," they are probably talking about the common stock of a company. Common stock is what the majority of investors and mutual funds hold in their investment accounts.

Now let's assume that Jim announces that things aren't going as well and the company hasn't sold many toys in the last few months. This would cause more people to want to sell their stock, believing something is wrong at Martin Toy Company, which would bring the price down. If enough people want out of the stock, that might cause the stock to drop from $24 a share to $12 a share. The $4 profit would be replaced by an $8 loss for each share owned! Because of this potential for loss, many investors can't stomach this kind of movement in share price, nor should they. Fortunately, there are other investments, such as mutual funds, which help ease the volatility that is often seen with individual stocks.

More Return Usually Means More Risk

In addition to common stock, companies sometimes offer a second class of ownership called "preferred stock." The "preferred" distinction doesn't necessarily mean that it is more desirable to investors, as when I say that "I prefer steak over chicken." In this case, the term "preferred" is used to refer to the preferential treatment that preferred stock shareholders get when it comes time for the company to distribute earnings to its shareholders. Preferred stock shareholders get their money *before* common stock shareholders. In exchange for this preferential treatment, preferred stock shareholders are limited in the return they get for each share they own. For example, they might receive up to 8% each year on their original investment. Common stock shareholders are willing to get in line behind the preferred stock shareholders because they get everything that is left over, which, as you might imagine, can be substantial.

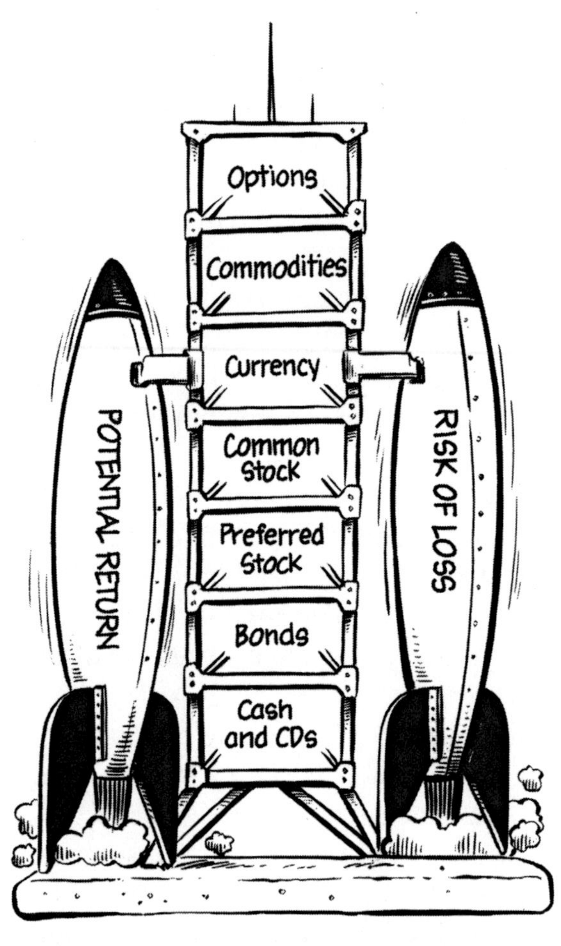

Preferential treatment can also be a good thing if the company runs into trouble. Let's say Martin's Toy Company has severe financial difficulties and is forced to file bankruptcy. All of Martin Toy Company's creditors, bondholders, and preferred stock shareholders would get paid before anyone holding common stock would see a dollar. Common stock shareholders get paid last when it comes to liquidation of the company. Often that means they get pennies on the dollar, even if everyone else has been paid in full. This is a real risk associated with individual stocks.

Secret #11: "The Skinny" on Fixed-Income Securities

Although the $44 trillion global stock market hogs our attention, the global bond market weighed in at $82 trillion in 2009 (according to the *Asset Allocation Adviser* in November of 2009). In addition to bonds, a variety of other fixed-income securities are often included in individual investors' investment portfolios. Let's look at some of them:

Fixed-income securities are often purchased by investors and their advisers to produce income. By controlling the amount of bonds and other fixed-income securities held in their clients' investment portfolios, money managers can also reduce volatility and risk.

Comparative Overview of Fixed-Income Securities

Less Risk 

	Commercial Paper	Preferred Stock	REITs	Bonds
What Is It?	Short-term IOU of nine months or less	Stock that gets a set rate of return instead of more upside	Trust that holds income-producing real estate	Formal contract for debt with a fixed "loan" period and a fixed rate of interest
Where Does It Come From?	Large, very well-rated, publicly-traded companies	Publicly-traded companies of all sizes and some private corporations	Some are publicly-traded and some are private	Companies and governments (city, county, state, federal, and foreign)
Easy to Buy/Sell?	Yes / Yes	Yes / Yes	Yes / No	Yes / Yes
Who Rates Them?	Standard & Poor's and Moody's	Standard & Poor's and Moody's	Forbes, Standard and Poor's, Morningstar	Standard & Poor's and Moody's
What Can Cause It to Go Down in Value?	Because it is such short-term debt, primarily company's financial strength	Company financial strength or ratings, interest rates, risk of being redeemed, or merger/acquisition of issuer	Quality of real estate portfolio, occupancy rates, and, inconsistent distributions	Company financial strength or ratings, interest rates, risk of being redeemed early, or merger/acquisition of issuer
Is the Return Fixed?	Interest rate is set when issued	It varies since the company can reduce, delay, or skip dividend payments	No, because dividends are from profit	Interest rate is normally set when issued

 **More Potential Return**

Bonds

A bond, in its simplest form, is a loan – a promise to pay back the principal along with a set amount of interest over a specific period of time. For example, a state may sell a bond in order to raise money to build a new bridge, while a company may sell a bond to get cash to buy a factory.

Bonds are generally considered less risky than stocks because they offer a steady stream of interest payments and the return of the original loan amount at the bond's maturity date. Less risk, however, does not equal no risk. If that company who issued bonds to buy the factory goes bankrupt, then all of their bondholders might end up only getting a part of their original investment. Of course, if this were to happen, the company's common stock shareholders might lose their entire investment.

Some bonds pay more interest than others because of two primary differences: the length to maturity and the perceived risk of default. If we hold all other things equal, it works like this:

- **Longer Bond Term Equals Higher Interest**
- **More Risk of Default Equals High Interest**

Let's say that a government wants to issue some new, long-term bonds, but the country has already racked up a serious amount of debt and is spending more than it is collecting in taxes. In order to get investors to buy their new bonds, the government will need to offer a higher interest rate to investors for the perceived higher level of risk. More debt equals more risk, which equals higher interest costs to the issuer (or the taxpayers).

A very common way to get into bonds is through a bond mutual fund. To reduce risk and to boost performance, bond fund managers keep their portfolios well-diversified by holding hundreds of individual bonds in a variety of different categories such as: corporate bonds, high-yield bonds, treasury bonds, municipal bonds, foreign bonds, and short, intermediate, or long-term bonds. Even though bond funds are still affected by changes in interest rates and overall economic conditions, individual investors can reduce the risks associated with owning individual bonds and still get the potential benefits of the bond market (we'll get to that in a minute).

Real Estate Investment Trusts (REITs)

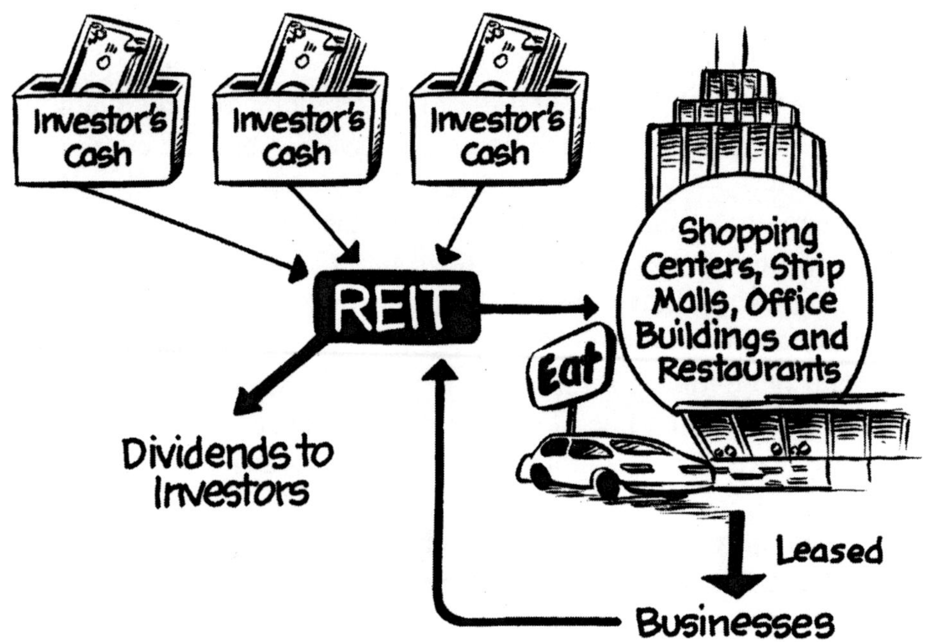

Another form of investment security that I would put in the fixed-income securities category is called a real estate investment trust, or a REIT (rhymes with "street"). The creator of the REIT gets investors to pool their money together in order to buy real estate property, which can be residential, commercial, or both. Income earned by the REIT is generated primarily by leasing the property owned by the REIT or from selling some of its properties. After deducting the REIT's expenses and management fees, the REIT will distribute most of the REIT's net income to its owners. REITs can produce a healthy income for their owners as long as the properties stay leased and continue to produce income. Depending on an investor's risk tolerance, income needs, and tax situation, REITs can have their place in a well-diversified portfolio. However, I would suggest caution when considering a privately-held REIT (one that hasn't gone "public" yet, meaning its units aren't bought and sold on a major exchange). While REITs are primarily purchased for long-term income, there are times when it could be necessary to liquidate a REIT. Over the years, I have found it very difficult for my clients to get out of private REITs. To avoid this problem, when building and managing my clients' investment portfolios, I prefer mutual funds and ETFs that specialize in holding a large basket of publicly-traded REITs.

Preferred Stocks

Preferred stock falls right under bonds and right above stock, which is why it was so creatively named "preferred stock." Unlike a bondholder, but like a common stockholder, investors in preferred stock have ownership in a corporation. Preferred shares commonly pay a dividend that is higher than that of common shares, but they don't usually have the voting rights or the potential for appreciation of common stock shares. Another difference between preferred stock and common stock becomes apparent if a company runs short on cash and cannot meet all of its obligations. The company must first pay bondholders their interest, next preferred stock shareholders get their dividends, and then common stock shareholders get what's left over. That means there can be times when a preferred stock shareholder won't receive any dividends at all.

Commercial Paper

Commercial paper is a form of unsecured debt typically used by very large, publicly-traded companies to help them meet their short-term obligations and routine operating expenses. Because the term is for nine months or less, the companies don't use the money to buy land, equipment, or buildings (bonds are for that). In other words, commercial paper is a formal IOU that big companies use to plug holes in their cash flows. Usually only companies with high credit ratings can issue their own commercial paper.

Generally, interest rates paid on commercial paper are usually higher than bonds issued by the same company. Commercial paper is not considered as secure as bonds, so naturally, investors demand a higher return for the higher risk. Commercial paper is purchased at a discount, and the face amount is paid to the investor at maturity (including principal and interest). While it is outstanding, however, the value of commercial paper will fluctuate based on the strength of the issuing company and changes in interest rates, just like the other fixed-income securities in this section.

According to a Federal Reserve report on commercial paper available online at the time of this writing (January 2011), more than 1,700 U.S. companies had commercial paper outstanding at the end of 2009. Commercial paper totaled $1.8 trillion at the end of 2007.

Looking for *Yield* in All the Wrong Places

Yield is what you earn on the money you invest. Investors can get into trouble when they seek yield without looking at the whole investment. If you earn 7% interest on a bond, but its price drops 11%, what did you really make for the year? That isn't a trick question. It is very important to keep in mind that a fixed-income security's price can be affected by both global and issuer specific factors after it has been sold to the public.

- Global factors would include changes in prevailing interest rates as well as the overall economic climate.

- Issuer specific factors would include changes in financial strength, changes in the amount of debt outstanding, the likelihood that the issuer will redeem the security early, the time left to maturity date, and the possibility of a merger or acquisition involving the issuer.

Buying a thirty-year bond when prevailing interest rates are low is an example of not looking at the whole investment and is probably not the best move for an individual investor. Yes, a thirty-year bond will pay more than a short-term alternative, but with rates likely to go up, you've just trapped yourself; the bond's value is very likely to go down substantially when rates start moving up. The investor would take a horrendous loss if he tried to move from the long-term bond into something with a higher interest rate (after rates had already moved up).

The allure of high yield bonds (also called junk bonds) can cause investors to overlook their risks. Yes, these bonds usually pay a higher yield than other bonds, but there is a reason for that; there's more risk of default. When a bond "defaults," that means that the issuers have stopped paying their semi-annual interest payments to bondholders and/or the bond becomes worthless. What good is a 9% yield on a junk bond if you never get all of your original investment back?

The bottom line is that we should weigh the interest to be earned against the potential loss of investment value.

Interest Rate Changes Have a Big Impact on Fixed-Income Securities

When the Federal Reserve raises interest rates to help rein in inflation, interest rates on fixed-income securities typically move in the same direction. New bonds and commercial paper start getting issued with the higher interest rates. All existing publicly-traded debt instruments get "re-priced" <u>immediately</u> by buyers and sellers in the market. Consequently, the price of existing fixed-income securities goes down, depending on the size of the interest rate increase.

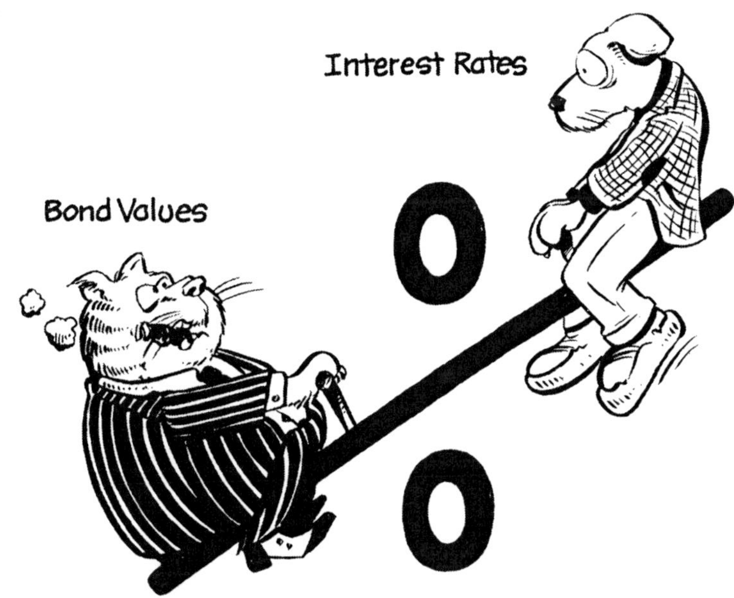

Let's say you own a $50,000 ten-year bond paying 5%. If interest rates increase by 1%, your bond will get re-priced by the market so that it would then be worth about $45,000. If interest rates go up another 1%, your bonds will fall further in value. This is because other investors could buy a "newer" bond that pays more interest than your bond does, so your bond would have to be *cheaper* so that its return to the buyer would be the same as what he or she would get on a "newer" bond. (Morningstar Research did a study on 10-year bonds and found that for every 1% increase in interest rates, bonds decreased by about 10%). We see the same thing with new cars. Even if it is <u>identical</u>, last year's car will drop in value as soon as the new ones roll onto the dealership lot.

Of course, if interest rates go down, the opposite change in value occurs; your bond is now worth more! In both scenarios, if you hold your bond to maturity, you will get the full face value of the bond no matter what interest rates have been doing.

Should Fixed-Income Securities Be Part of Your Investment Portfolio?

Okay, with all this about fixed-income securities, the important question is, "should they be in your investment portfolio?" The straightforward answer is "yes." How much, of course, depends on your situation.

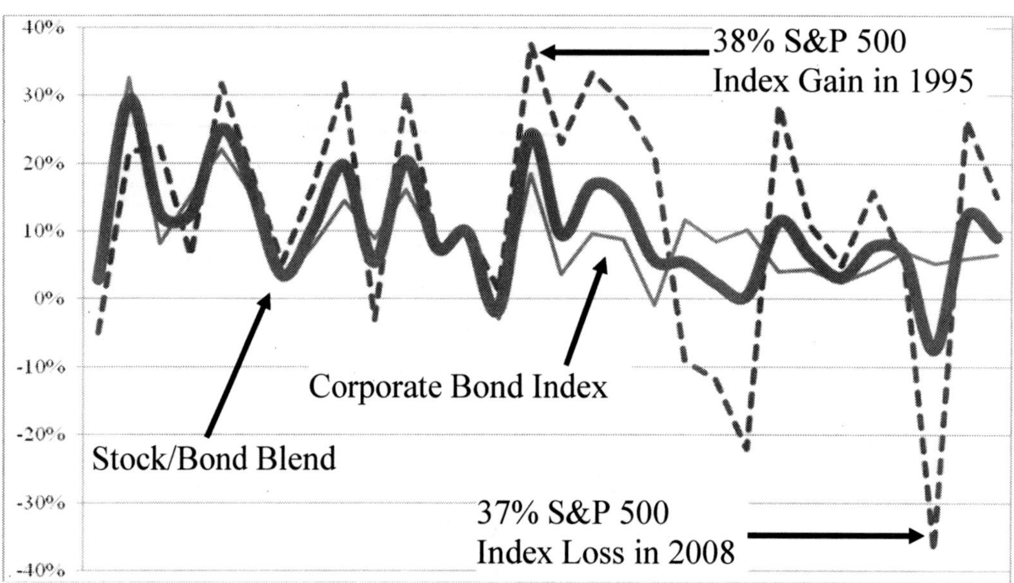

The dashed line on the chart above is the raw performance of the S&P 500 index (dividends, gains, but no fees or taxes) for the 30-year period of 1981 through 2010. Annual returns swung widely to as high as a 38% gain in 1995 to as low as a 37% loss in 2008. For the same period, annual returns for investment grade corporate bonds are represented by the thin, solid line (Lehman Brothers then Barclays bond index). The highest gain for bonds was 33% in 1982, and the biggest loss was 3% in 1994 (interest and appreciation, but no fees or tax).

Common sense would say that an investment portfolio built with <u>both</u> stocks and bonds ought to be less volatile than a portfolio made up entirely of stocks. For example, a 70/30 blend of bonds to stocks produces the smoother, thicker line you also see on the graph for the same period. Of course, the next thirty years may look absolutely nothing like the last thirty years, but the potential for bonds and other fixed-income securities to dampen the volatility of a stock portfolio is hard to ignore.

Secret #12: Mutual Funds as Part of Your Retirement Plan

Maintaining a diversified portfolio can be quite time consuming. Keeping up with each holding and ensuring the right amount of risk is being taken is too much work for most people. This is why the majority of investors purchase mutual funds to gain exposure to the stock market. A mutual fund is a large pool of money created by many investors coming together to invest in stocks, bonds, and other securities. Mutual funds are one of the most common investments found in brokerage accounts.

- ✓ In January 2011, there were over 26,000 mutual funds according to Morningstar Research.
- ✓ The *2009 ICI Fact Book* reports that 73% of IRAs held mutual funds in 2008.
- ✓ According to eHow.com, on February 21, 2011, the worldwide total in mutual funds was estimated to be $25 trillion.

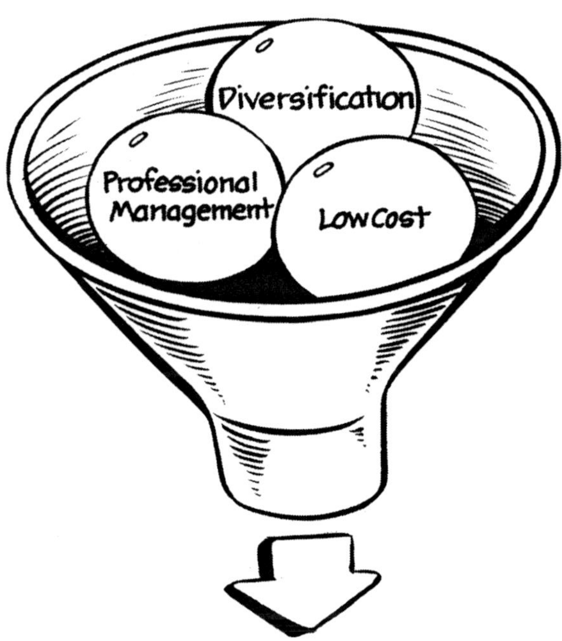

Why are mutual funds so popular? In addition to flexibility and ease of withdrawals, mutual funds offer access to professional money management and diversification at a relatively low cost.

Mutual Funds Are like Investment Shopping Carts

- Fund managers push their shopping carts through the aisles of the "stock" market.
- Research analysts help the manager decide which companies are a "good buy."
- Fund managers bring their shopping lists with them each time they go to the stock market so they know what to buy. This is called the mutual fund prospectus.
- Each mutual fund is a separate shopping cart. Some fund managers are responsible for more than one cart. Fund managers often buy the same companies.
- Some mutual fund carts only hold stocks of companies in specific industries like healthcare or technology, small companies, or international companies.
- Some fund managers are more active with buying and selling what's in their carts, while others are more passive and only make a few changes to what's in their carts each year.
- If the shopping cart gets too full, the fund manager will sell companies back to the stock market, where other fund managers and individual investors will buy them.
- Individual investors buy part of the mutual fund, and that gives the fund manager *grocery money* to buy more stuff for his cart.
- The value of each mutual fund shopping cart depends on the value of everything inside it. Overall volatility and movement of the stock market also affect its value.
- Some mutual funds *carts* have toppled over because they had lousy securities or the manager made large bets on risky companies. Mutual funds are not guaranteed or insured by the FDIC.

So What Do They Have to Say for Themselves?

Each fund issues a prospectus, a lengthy document *written by attorneys for attorneys*, which outlines the funds' guidelines and objectives in excruciating detail. If you can get through it, you'll find insight into how the fund will be managed and what type of investments it will hold. Often times, websites such as Morningstar or the mutual fund company itself, will provide easy to understand graphs and information about the fund.

Where Do You Get Mutual Funds?

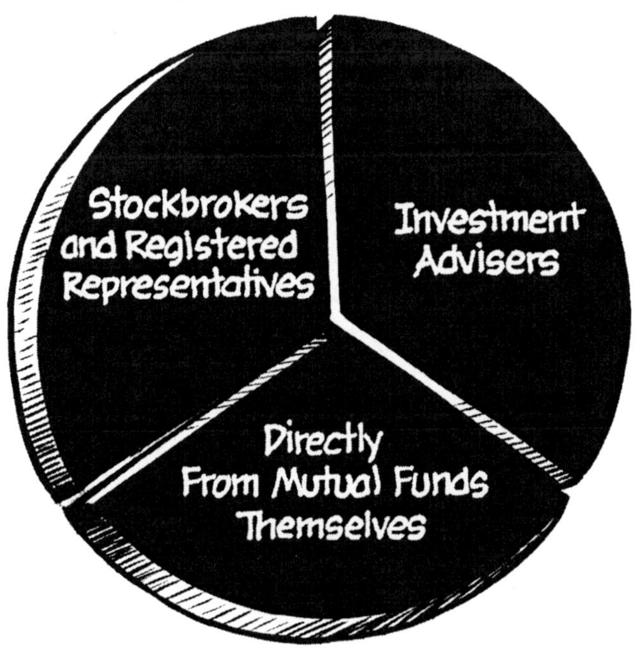

One of the great things about mutual funds is you can decide whether you want help picking and managing them, or would rather choose the funds yourself. You can buy them from a stockbroker, buy them directly from the mutual funds, or hire an investment adviser to buy them for you.

Do-It-Yourself: If you have the time, the interest, and the expertise, you can build your own investment portfolio and select mutual funds for yourself. Some online brokerage firms, such as Fidelity, have tools to help you make your selection. You can also contact the mutual funds directly. Mutual funds that work directly with the investor are called "no-load" mutual funds, because they don't pay a broker a commission to distribute them. No load mutual funds, like Vanguard, hire their own brokers to work with investors directly, usually over the phone.

Buy from a Broker: Stockbrokers and registered representatives regularly recommend what are called "load" mutual funds. It is important to note that securities regulations require that stockbrokers make suitable mutual fund recommendations to investors. Brokers receive commissions for selling these mutual funds to their customers. The "load" refers to a sales charge that is incurred by the investor in one of three ways:

1. Deducted from what the investor contributes (called an "A" share);
2. Deducted in the form of higher annual fund fees plus a surrender charge if the investor leaves the fund early (called a "B" share); or
3. Deducted in the form of higher annual fund fees (called a "C" share).

Hire an Adviser: Investment advisers can typically be hired for 1 to 2% per year to manage your investment account. Technically, the individual professional is called an investment adviser representative and the firm is called a Registered Investment Adviser, or RIA. Most investment advisers use no load mutual funds when building an investment portfolio for their clients. Sometimes they will also include load funds, but the investment adviser can get them "at cost" without the applied sales charge; the load fund is then referred to as being "load-waived." It is important to note that lines have blurred over the years between these different purchase options. For example, some stockbrokerage firms can also act as an investment adviser.

What Do Mutual Funds Cost?

The fund managers themselves charge a daily fee for their services. This "expense ratio" is typically expressed as an annual percentage of the assets in the mutual fund. For example, if a fund charges 1% per year and you have $10,000 in that fund, you are paying $100 per year for the fund manager to pick your stocks and bonds inside that fund. You will never see this charge on your investment statements. It is deducted daily by the mutual fund out of what they make or lose for the day. Just like anything you buy, the cheapest isn't always the best, nor is the most expensive.

How to Pick from 26,000 Mutual Fund Choices

With so many choices, most fee-based investment advisers will use a screening process to come up with a short list of acceptable mutual funds for their clients' portfolios. Without educating my competitors too much, here are some of the criteria we use at my investment firm:

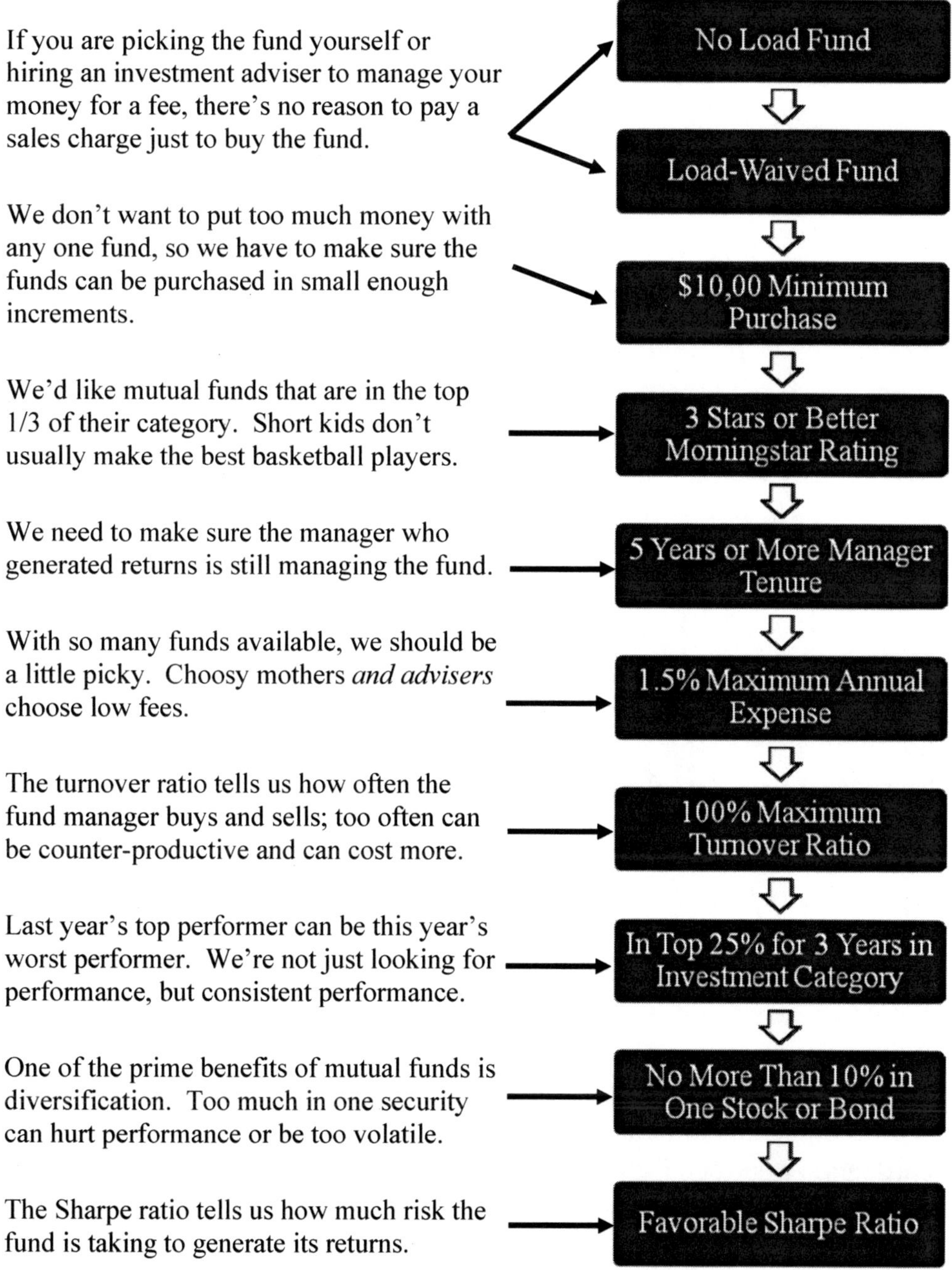

Almost, But Not Quite Mutual Funds

Some investments look a lot like open-ended mutual funds, but are completely different. Here are some examples:

Variable Annuity Subaccounts

Variable annuities are a security product offered by insurance companies. They are designed primarily to provide the opportunity for tax-deferred growth through investments inside the annuity, which are called subaccounts. The insurance company enters into an agreement with mutual fund managers to manage the subaccounts. For example, Fidelity, Vanguard, and American Funds offer mutual funds. They also offer subaccounts inside variable annuities that are very similar to the mutual funds these companies also manage. Even though more people invest in mutual funds, variable annuities are big business. According to the *National Underwriter's* online publication in March of 2009, about $120 billion goes into variable annuities each year.

Unit Investment Trusts (UIT)

UITs make an initial public offering (IPO) just like a company would when it first sells shares of its stock. Unit investment trusts are not managed by a portfolio manager as are mutual or hedge funds. They typically hold a large number of various types of bonds or other assets, but are rarely diversified. Whatever is purchased when the trust is established will be held for the specified duration of the fund.

Closed-End Funds

Like a UIT, a closed-end fund raises a fixed amount of capital through an IPO and is then traded on stock exchanges. However, unlike a UIT, a closed-end fund does have a portfolio manager who buys and sells securities and typically focuses on a specific industry or country. The largest difference between a closed-end fund and a regular mutual fund is that it has a set amount of shares, while the typical mutual fund (which is technically called an "open-ended fund") can continually issue new shares of itself to the public. An advantage of a closed-end version is that the manager doesn't have to liquidate holdings at possibly a bad time in order to redeem shares for shareholders. A regular mutual fund manager may have to sell holdings in order to meet share redemption requests.

Exchange-Traded Funds (ETF)

With lower fees than mutual funds and the precision to invest in a specific area of the market, exchange-traded funds have increased in popularity. For example, if we wanted to capitalize on the movements in the energy sector, we might buy an ETF that invests only in that specific sector. The majority of ETFs are considered passive investments because they are designed to mirror the movements of a specific stock index. Once the portfolio is built, there's not much for a fund manager to do, so investors don't have to worry or be concerned with a fund manager's stock-buying and stock-selling skills. As of 2008, there were 728 ETFs that held $531 billion in investments (*ICI Fact Book*, Section 7, 2009).

Secret #13: Investment and Financial Product Fees

Besides the fees you might pay for an adviser to manage your portfolio, there are also investment and product fees. Sometimes these fees translate directly into what the adviser gets, and sometimes the adviser gets none of the fees. In other words, what the investor pays in fees often has little to do with what the adviser is paid. You will understand the different fees and the disconnection that I am referring to once you finish this chapter. Knowledge is power, and you're about to be all charged up.

Investment Custodian Fees: It is not unusual for brokerage firms to charge an annual fee for each account they hold, especially on IRAs and inactive accounts with little or no trading. This fee might range from $25 to $50 per year. Sometimes investors think that this is all they are paying to have their accounts "handled" by the brokerage firm. Even though these fees may not seem like a significant cost, I've included a discussion of custodian fees in this chapter for this very reason. If you think that $25 or $50 is all you are paying, look again. Mutual funds have fees. Variable annuities have fees. Securities have transaction costs. If properly licensed, stockbrokers can also charge a fee as an investment adviser.

Action Item: No one's going to do anything for $50 a year. Make sure you understand your fees. Ask the adviser, "How am I paying for your services? How do you get paid on my accounts?"

Brokerage Transaction Fees: Since investors cannot sell securities directly to other investors on the stock exchanges, consumers have to go through a broker-dealer to buy and sell securities. Whether they buy and sell securities through a stockbroker or a discount broker, consumers will usually pay the broker-dealer a transaction fee for their brokerage service (that's the "broker" part of being a broker-dealer). Transaction costs vary substantially, depending on the security being bought or sold, how many shares are being bought or sold, and the fee schedule used by the particular broker-dealer. Trades that are placed by individuals or by investment advisers online usually cost less than trades placed by stockbrokers.

Action Item: Before you ask a stockbroker or an investment adviser to place trades in your investment account, ask for a copy of the broker-dealer's fee schedule.

Dealer Markup: Few retail investors know about the profit or loss that broker-dealers experience when they sell securities to their customers from their own portfolio. This is the "dealer" part of being a broker-dealer. In a "dealer" capacity, a broker-dealer is said to be acting as a "principal" in the transaction.

Let's say that the broker-dealer firm owns a stock that it bought for $20 a share. If they sell it to you from their own inventory for $25 per share, they would make $5 a share. Likewise, if they sell it to you for $15 per share, the broker-dealer firm would lose $5 a share.

If it is going to cost you the same amount per share whether you buy the stock from the broker-dealer or on the open market, what difference does it make? Why should you care if they make or lose $5 per share on the trade if you are paying the same price either way? Seems harmless enough, right? Here's how you can tell if there is a problem: whose idea is it to buy the stock, the stockbroker's or yours?

If it is your idea, then I don't see a problem. Broker-dealers will markup the transaction based on the current price at the time of the transaction. There are also rules that broker-dealers have to follow as to how much they can mark up the transaction. Larger markups usually occur with penny or speculative stocks.

Now here's where it gets tricky. What if it is the stockbroker's idea? Let's make sure we've got this straight: *the stockbroker is recommending that you buy the stock, presumably because it will go up in value. If that's true, then why would the broker-dealer firm be willing to sell it from their inventory? If it is so good, you'd think the broker-dealer would be buying more of it, not selling what the firm already owns to you.* Does that make sense to you? It doesn't to me. Common sense would tell us that there is something not right about this situation.

Action Item: Each time a stockbroker recommends you buy a security, ask if his firm will be acting as a broker (securities agent) or dealer (principal) in the transaction, <u>before you do anything.</u>

The potential conflicts with dealer markups can be avoided in two ways:

1. Get your stock picks from a broker-dealer firm that only serves in a broker capacity, not as a dealer in their own inventory.

2. Hire an investment adviser to manage your portfolio for a fee, and move the account to a discount brokerage firm. If your investment adviser buys a stock for your account, it doesn't matter who the seller is because the investment adviser is only paid a fee by you.

Mutual Fund Fees: There is a wide range of fees charged to the investor by the different types of mutual funds. This fee is usually based on the way the mutual fund is sold or distributed to investors. Shown below are some of the most popular fund share classes:

- **A-share funds**: This fund type has two main costs: a one-time, front-end charge to get in, which pays the broker for selling the fund to the investor, and the annual expense charge, which is what the mutual fund charges for its management of the investor's money. The more you put into one mutual fund family, the lower the front-end charge will be for an A-share fund (consequently, the broker's commission percentage will also be reduced).

- **B-share funds**: These funds don't have a front-end charge, but still pay the broker for selling the fund to the investor. 100% of the investor's money goes into the fund, but for five to seven years, the mutual fund charges a higher expense ratio in order to recoup what it paid the broker for the sale. If you leave the fund early, you pay a surrender charge.

- **C-share funds**: These funds always stay about 1% higher in fees than A-shares because the broker is paid that 1% each year.

- **No-load funds**: For years, "no charges to get in or out" and "just an expense ratio" have been what set no-load funds apart from other mutual fund types. For this reason, no-load funds are purchased primarily by individual investors, as well as fee-based investment advisers and money managers.

Some Annuities Have Fees and Some Don't.

Immediate Annuities have no fees. The immediate annuity buyer exchanges a lump sum of cash for a lifetime of income. There are no surrender fees because immediate annuities cannot be surrendered. At the death of the owner, payments stop and the insurance company keeps the remaining premium. Some companies offer a "cash refund" option that guarantees that the heirs will get what has not been paid out from the original amount, but of course, that reduces the lifetime income payments to the annuity owner while he or she is alive.

Fixed Rate Annuities do not have fees. The insurance company pays interest on the money that the owner invests. This works much like a CD. CDs don't have fees; the interest is already netted for the bank's expenses. The same is true for the interest credited by the insurance company.

Fixed Index Annuities do not have fees. Even though the principal invested remains secure, the insurance company pays a variable rate of interest that is based on how a stock market index performs over a year's time (hence the name "fixed"). If there is no increase in the stock market index, there is no interest credited. Fixed interest rate options are also available.

Variable Annuities have two types of fees: **insurance charges,** which typically run 1.25 to 1.75% per year and **investment fees**, which usually cost 0.5 to 1.5% per year. Fees vary considerably across companies and individual products. All in all, a variable annuity can cost 1.75 to 3.25% per year.

Optional Annuity Riders: Fixed and variable annuities have a variety of optional features that are called "riders." They are available at an extra charge and can "ride" on top of the base annuity. For example, if you want the annuity to guarantee a lifetime of income, you might opt for an "income rider." A 0.2 to 1.5% fee would be added to the annuity.

Surrender Fees: Most annuities have surrender fees between 7 and 10% that go away after 5 to 10 years. These charges usually do not apply at the death of the owner. State insurance departments must approve the surrender charges, fees, and features of the annuities sold in their state.

Section IV

Banking and Insurance as Part of Your Retirement Plan

Secret #14: Should You Bank on Your Bank?

Can you count on your bank? It's a natural concern when we saw a total of 297 banks fail in 2009 and 2010, in contrast to just 50 bank failures in the previous eight years (www.fdic.org). Let's dive right into this subject with six important questions:

1. **How do banks make money?** Banks pay interest on CDs, money market accounts, and savings accounts (deposits). Then, they loan that deposited money out to other individuals and businesses to finance cars, boats, houses, and business assets. The bank pays less interest than it charges, so it makes money on the spread. Let's say a bank has $100 million in deposits and loans out 80% of that. If they earn 5% on the loans, they'll get $4,000,000 in loan interest. If they pay 2% interest on the $100 million in customer deposits, that costs the bank $2,000,000. So, the bank can then use the remaining $2,000,000 to pay their expenses (personnel, office space, and bad loans) and to make a profit.

2. **What other services do banks offer?** Over the years, some banks have expanded beyond their traditional business model to offer non-bank financial services, such as insurance and securities products. To offer insurance products (fixed annuities, life insurance, and long-term care), the bank instructs its personnel to become properly licensed in their state. To offer securities products (like variable annuities, stocks, bonds, and mutual funds), the bank's personnel must be securities licensed and registered as representatives of a broker-dealer. The FDIC does not insure insurance and securities products.

3. **Why were there so many failures in 2009 and 2010?** The answer is three words: *real estate loans.* When the real estate market bubble popped and the recession arrived, many banks found themselves with large amounts of residential and commercial loans tied to real estate. Businesses that went belly up and people who lost their jobs couldn't make loan payments. Banks' resources were squeezed. Losses mounted. Capital shrank. New loans were harder to make because of declining availability of consumer credit and declining real estate values.

4. **Is there anything you can do to protect yourself in the event your bank fails?** Yes, don't put more than $250,000 into each account you have at a bank; that will keep you under the FDIC insurance limit.

5. **How do you monitor your bank?** Visit www.bankrate.com where analysts assign banks one to five star ratings based on their financial strength. The analysts provide detailed reports that include key financial data and an explanation of why banks receive their individual star ratings. The fdic.gov website is also an excellent source of financial data about your bank. It is difficult to navigate, so follow these steps carefully:

    - Click on "Regulations & Examinations"
    - Click on "Required Financial Reports"
    - Select "Call and Thrift Reports"
    - Click "Call Report a Thrift Financial Report Data"
    - Select "View or Download Data"
    - Select Report Type: Uniform Bank Performance Report
    - Type in the bank's name and then click generate report (two key sections you'll want to look at are the bank's income statement and balance sheet).

6. **What happens when a bank fails?** The state steps in and temporarily closes the bank. In Florida, for example, the Office of Financial Regulation fulfills this role. Next, the FDIC is appointed the receiver. That means that the FDIC takes over the bank's assets and liabilities and assumes the duty of selling assets and paying debts, including claims for deposits in excess of the insured limit. The FDIC then finds and negotiates with a strong bank to take over the failed bank. Based on the terms of the deal, the FDIC then injects some cash in the deal to make it work for the new bank, and more importantly, to make sure depositors are protected. Customers of the failed bank automatically become customers of the new bank.

Secret #15: Insurance Companies: Big Buildings, Lots of Money

Insurance companies are known for having big buildings downtown and a lot of money, and here's why that is a good thing: our American way of life is built on our ability to transfer the risk of major financial events to someone else. Unfortunately, because they are engaged in class warfare, some politicians would love for us to hate insurance companies. I would sincerely like to know how each of the following would get done without the insurance industry:

- How would banks make home loans? What if the house burns down? Now what? How does it get rebuilt?
- How many chickens would it cost for the doctor to deliver a baby?
- How would injured workers get paid for not working?
- How would families survive (financially) after a wrongful death?
- How many young adults would be able to afford a replacement vehicle after an automobile accident?

You get my point. We need insurance companies, and we need them to be big and strong. Some people think they're wasting money on insurance if they don't have to file a claim. When you buy an insurance policy, you're protecting something of value. Never having to file a claim is a blessing.

Personally, if I never had to undergo six hours of surgery for two crushed discs in my neck in 2005, it would have been fine with me! I would have been happy to pay monthly health insurance premiums without ever filing a claim.

What Is an Insurance Company?

Basically, insurance involves a group of people agreeing to share risks. It is a very old idea, which started back when sailing ships were destroyed or lost their cargos at sea. To protect themselves from total ruin, the merchants got clever and divided their cargos among several boats. That way, if one of the boats was destroyed, no merchant lost everything. Each stood to lose only a small portion (Insurance Institute of Michigan). In much the same way, individuals and businesses can protect themselves from large losses by paying premiums to an insurance company.

What Do Insurance Companies Do?

Today, there are many forms of insurance; life, health, home, and auto insurance are just a few. When you buy insurance, you join many others who pay money to an insurance company. The insurance company uses the money they collect to pay claims submitted by those insured by their policies.

An insurance policy is a financial contract between a policyholder (the insured) and an insurance company (the insurer). The insurer agrees to pay in the event that the person or property insured suffers the loss that is specified in the policy. For example, a homeowner's policy would pay for the damage sustained to your home because of a fire. Insurance companies also issue life insurance policies to address the costs, or loss of income, that the beneficiary may face when their loved one dies.

What Is the Difference Between Public Versus Private Insurance?

The Medicare and Medicaid programs are good examples of public run insurance plans. They are administered and overseen by the federal government, which taxes the population to fund these public plans. This presents a real cost to both the economy and taxpayers. Profit-seeking insurance companies provide a wide range of consumer choices because they compete on the basis of price, quality, and customer service.

What Are the Different Types of Insurance Companies?

- Property & casualty insurance companies focus on auto, homeowners, businesses, and liability types of insurance.

- Life insurance companies focus on life insurance, disability insurance, long-term care, and annuities.

In most countries, life and non-life insurers are subject to different regulatory, tax, and accounting rules. The main reason for the distinction between the two types of companies is that life and annuity products are long-term in nature. By contrast, non-life insurance usually covers a shorter period, such as one year.

How Are Insurance Companies Regulated?

For the most part, insurance company regulation is left to individual states as the result of the federal McCarran-Ferguson Act. The McCarran-Ferguson Act was passed after the U.S. Supreme Court ruled that insurance companies were subject to federal antitrust and price-fixing laws. However, Congress overruled the Supreme Court's decision and exempted insurance companies from federal regulation.

Under state laws, insurance departments are responsible for creating licensing requirements for insurance companies, in addition to maintaining standards for insurance brokers and agents. Insurance regulatory departments have the authority to investigate insurance complaints and impose fines and other punishments, including suspending or revoking authorization to do business in the state. For example, in the State of Florida, the Office of Insurance Regulations assumes the primary responsibility for regulation, compliance, and enforcement of statutes related to insurance markets.

If you ever feel that you've been unfairly denied payment of a legitimate claim, or if you believe that your insurance agent has misrepresented a policy to you, first call the insurance company. If they cannot or will not help you, file a complaint with the state insurance department.

What Is the Business of Insurance Companies?

Principally, insurance companies pool funds from many individuals to pay for the losses that some may suffer. Each insured person is protected for a specified, known fee that can be budgeted and paid instead of being subjected to a potentially catastrophic loss. Insurance companies are good at measuring the risk of loss. The most common risks they insure are auto, home, life, health, casualty, property, and professional liability. Other forms of coverage could include aviation, builder's risk, credit, crop, earthquake, flood, marine, terrorism, volcano, and windstorm. Many insurance companies are also involved in other businesses, such as banking, commercial real estate, and investment management.

How Do Insurance Companies Make Money?

To issue an insurance policy, an insurance company charges a premium, which is the primary source of insurance company revenue. They also pay out money for claims and benefits under the policies they issue. Insurance companies are very good at predicting how many losses they'll have in a given year. They can set the proper premium cost by estimating the claims expected for the year, along with their operating expenses, so that ultimately, they can make a profit.

Here's an example: if a policyholder pays $700 in homeowners' insurance premiums each year, but does not have a claim, the insurance company gets to keep the $700. Likewise, if a policyholder pays $700 in homeowners' insurance premiums and has a fire that causes $20,000 in damage, the insurance company will pay out $20,000 even though the policyholder has only paid $700 in premium.

Insurance companies also make money on their reserves. To the contrary of what many consumers think, insurance company reserves are not typically held idle in a savings account or put into ultra risky, exotic investments. Instead, most insurance companies have their own investment departments to carefully invest those reserves. It is certainly worth their time. If the insurance company makes a positive return on those investments, then that money adds to their profits (or helps to reduce losses if they've had a worse-than-expected amount of claims). For example, if the company makes a 6% return on $50 million in reserves, they could add an extra $3 million to their bottom line.

Do Insurance Companies Have Insurance for Themselves?

One way insurance companies manage the risks they take is through reinsurance. The insurance company (insurer) enters into an agreement with another insurance company (reinsurer) to transfer some of its exposure to large claims. The reinsurer agrees to absorb some of the insurer's losses in exchange for a reinsurance premium. With reinsurance, the insurer can then issue policies with higher limits and take on more risk because some of that risk is now transferred to the reinsurer.

How Safe Is Your Money with an Insurance Company?

In 2008 and 2009, there was a wave of negative newspaper stories about banks, mortgage companies, brokerage firms, and insurance companies. It was a difficult period for everyone. However, insurance companies are in little danger of experiencing the failure rate of banks. According to a January 2011 article from the National Association of Fixed Annuities (www.nafa.com), only 30 insurance companies were deemed insolvent, versus 2,982 banks, during the period of 1983 through 2010.

Are Insurance Companies Rated? Do They Get a Health Score?

Choosing the right insurance company is just as important as choosing the right type of insurance coverage. It doesn't do much good to buy a policy from a company that won't be around or that will have trouble paying the claims and benefits offered by a policy. That's why many consumers and most insurance advisers look to the independent evaluations of rating agencies, such as A.M. Best, Standard & Poor's, and Moody's. Each rating service evaluates the financial strength and claims-paying ability of the insurer and the risks that could affect their long-term survival. Before you make a final decision about your insurance company, you should know their financial ratings. Here's a summary of the ratings:

> **A.M. Best** Company's financial strength rating is an independent opinion, based on a comprehensive quantitative and qualitative evaluation of a company's balance sheet strength, operating performance, and business profile. The top four ratings are A++ (Superior), A+ (Superior), A (Excellent), and A- (Excellent). www.ambest.com
>
> The analysts at **Standard & Poor's** provide financial strength ratings for insurance companies based on each company's ability to meet the terms of its insurance policies and contracts. The top four ratings are AAA (Extremely Strong), AA (Very Strong), A (Strong), and BBB (Good). www.standardandpoors.com
>
> **Moody's** ratings provide investors with a simple grading system for measuring insurance company creditworthiness. Nine symbols are

used to designate the level of credit risk from lowest risk to greatest risk: Aaa, Aa, A, Baa, Ba, B, Caa, Ca, and C. www.moodys.com

Can Insurance Companies Fail? What Happens?

State insurance departments closely monitor insurance companies. The states are responsible for protecting policyholders from the risks of insurance company financial failure. Insurance companies are required to keep substantial sums of cash and short term investments on hand to pay policy claims. They are also not allowed to buy investments on borrowed money. The investing must be done with actual dollars, and regulations restrict the types of investments that can be made.

When an insurance company is unable to meet its financial responsibilities, the insurance commissioner determines if the financial issues can be resolved by the insurance company. The state attempts to rehabilitate the troubled insurance company, but if rehabilitation will not work, the commissioner declares the company to be insolvent. The state then takes control of the insurance company and assigns a receiver to account for and liquidate all assets. The state then distributes the cash to the creditors who have a valid claim. If there aren't enough assets to pay policyholders back, the state insurance guaranty association may need to step in to make up the difference. A state life and health insurance guaranty association has been created in each of the 50 states to protect the policyholders of an insolvent insurance company. All insurance companies who are licensed to sell life, health, or annuity products in a state must be members of the state's guaranty association to protect policyholders should a company fail.

The insurance coverage, benefits, and guarantees offered by insurance companies are only as good as the insurance company itself. If you are working with financial professionals, ask them to give you reports on the financial strength and ratings of the company they are recommending. If you are doing the research yourself, be sure to check the investments and reserves maintained by the company and look up their ratings. You may also want to call the State Department of Insurance to verify whether the company is licensed in your state or has had any complaints filed against it. Your state can also provide information on the guaranty association coverage limits that apply in the event of insurance company failure.

Secret #16: The Proper Use of Life Insurance

We must have made a wrong turn in Albuquerque! What is a chapter about life insurance doing in a book about retirement planning? Trillions of dollars, that's what. Life insurance and other financial products from insurance companies play an **enormous** role in the lives of millions of Americans, both <u>before</u> and <u>after</u> retirement. The five primary financial products offered by insurance companies include:

- ✓ Health insurance
- ✓ Disability insurance
- ✓ Life insurance
- ✓ Long-term care insurance
- ✓ Annuities

Although health and disability insurance serve a vital role in the finances of many Americans, please note that I am deliberately omitting them from our discussion. These insurance products are primarily obtained through employer-based group plans and they are not really part of retirement planning.

Life Insurance

By paying the premiums each year, a life insurance policy owner can designate a lump sum to be paid to beneficiaries at his or her death. According to the *U.S. Census Bureau, Statistical Abstract of the United States, 2011*, **there were 335 million policies in the United States at the end of 2008, totaling $19.1 trillion dollars of life insurance**. Whoa.

I have advised clients since 1993 about proper use and selection of life insurance. Life insurance has several notable benefits:

1. A small annual premium can produce a large death benefit.
2. The death benefit comes exactly when it is needed.
3. Death proceeds are not normally taxable to the beneficiary.
4. Death proceeds to a beneficiary are not subject to probate.
5. In many states, life insurance policies are not subject to the claims of creditors (please consult an attorney in your specific state).

Reasons People Buy Life Insurance

1. **Death of the *Breadwinner***: It is not hard to determine the proper amount of life insurance needed for an individual's situation. You just need to add together two numbers:

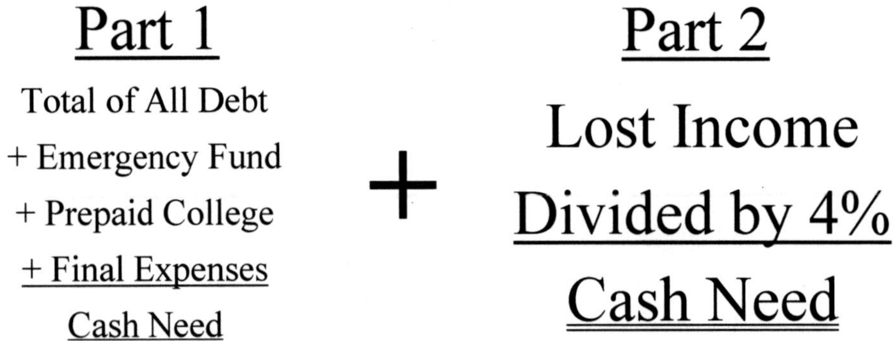

Part 1: How much do you owe on your cars, house, boat, credit cards, and business loans? Are there children or grandchildren who will need financial support for their college education? How much cash do you need to establish a decent emergency fund based on your circumstances and lifestyle? How much will you need to handle the final expenses of the deceased (i.e., medical bills, funeral expenses, and legal bills)? Perhaps, there's a total need for $200,000 to take care of one-time expenses.

Part 2: How much income will be lost if the *breadwinner* dies? Take that number and divide by 4%, and you'll have the cash lump sum that will be needed to replace the lost income. If the *breadwinner* dies, the lump sum then goes to work (by being invested) to provide the lost income. For example: $40,000 of lost income, divided by 4%, equals a $1,000,000 lump sum.

To get the total amount of life insurance needed, we simply add together Part 1 and Part 2, which would be $1,200,000 in this example. This formula can also be used by retirees to determine whether they need to keep their existing life insurance policies or if those polices can be surrendered or converted to retirement income. Situations will vary considerably, but this is a good starting point.

Reasons People Buy Life Insurance

2. **Pay-off Debt or Secure a Loan**: Many people do not want to leave their survivors in debt, so they buy life insurance. The husband of one of my clients recently died. He had wisely purchased a life insurance policy that was big enough to pay-off their mortgage. Despite her grief, my client was comforted by his prudent planning, which left her unburdened by a mortgage for the rest of her life.

   Life insurance is often required as one of the conditions of a bank loan. In 2010, I consolidated my financial and investment offices into one permanent location in Ormond Beach, Florida. We completely remodeled the second floor of an existing building to suit our needs. As you can imagine, the costs were significant, so we made arrangements with a local bank to cover the costs of the demolition and reconstruction. As part of the financing package, the bank required life insurance on me in an amount equal to the loan, just in case I didn't live long enough to see the loan repaid.

3. **Fund the Buy-Sell Agreements between Business Partners**: Most buy-sell agreements will call for the purchase of life insurance on each business partner by the other business partner. This assures that money is available for the surviving partner to buy the deceased partner's share of the business from his heirs. (Without an agreement and life insurance in place, a business owner might find himself with an unexpected new partner, his previous partner's widow!) Term insurance is often used because it is relatively cheap. The cost is considered by many to be a prudent expenditure.

4. **Pension Maximization**: One of the biggest decisions that some lucky retirees get to make is how they will take their pensions. Often, they have a choice between getting payments for a single lifetime or for a joint lifetime with their spouse. The joint pension is obviously better for the spouse, but that monthly check can be a lot less than the single pension amount. Unless there is a health condition that threatens to shorten the life of one of the spouses, the single versus joint pension decision can be a tough one to make.

   If the pensioner (the retiring employee who is entitled to the pension) is healthy, life insurance may be a viable solution. This two-part "pension maximization" strategy calls for the pensioner to take the single life pension *and also buy* a life insurance policy with some of the "extra" pension income that is coming in from the higher single life payment. The net pension is higher, even after deducting the cost of the life insurance. In the event the pensioner dies early, the spouse gets the insurance. Sometimes this strategy will work and sometimes it will not; it is critical to run the numbers both ways to see which way works best. If the pensioner is in bad health or young, this approach may not be the best option.

5. **Transfer Wealth to the Next Generation**: There are many well-established financial strategies that can help families reduce income and estate taxes so that more money can be transferred from one generation to the next. Some of these use life insurance. Here is just one example:

   > Let's say a father has a $100,000 IRA that he wants to leave to his daughter. He's 71 and is taking required minimum distributions each year. If the father turns the IRA into a guaranteed lifetime incomc, he can buy a life insurance policy for $250,000 with the after-tax income. When he dies, the daughter will get the $250,000 income tax-free; however, if instead the father left the IRA to his daughter, the IRA would have been treated as taxable incomc on top of all of her other income. I'll take tax-free over taxable-at-my-highest-tax-bracket any day of the week! How about you?

Choosing Between Term and Permanent Life Insurance

A common question involving life insurance is whether someone should buy term or permanent life insurance. While there are those who are adamant about buying term or permanent, it actually depends on each individual's situation. Some people should get term insurance and some should get permanent insurance.

Term insurance provides coverage for a certain amount of time and for a specified annual cost. Two popular choices are 10-year term and 20-year term. The annual premium for a 10-year term policy is fixed and does not change during the 10-year period; after the 10 years, the premium will increase. Likewise, for a 20-year term policy, the annual premium is set and will not increase for the 20-year period. Then it jumps substantially.

Here's a real life example that I know a lot about: as part of my own personal planning, my wife, Toni, owns a 10-year term policy on me that costs about $1,500 each year. If I were to die during this 10-year period, she would collect the resulting life insurance proceeds. While I have other life insurance, the purpose of this particular 10-year term policy is to provide an extra level of protection for my family during this 10-year period (while I am building assets, paying down debt, and the children are young). At the end of the 10-year period, we will evaluate whether or not we need to continue this policy. My situation illustrates the purpose of term insurance: to provide a large amount of life insurance coverage at a low cost for a specified number of years.

Permanent Insurance is used when the need for life insurance coverage is, well, permanent. Here's an example: let's say a 55-year-old couple, for whatever reason, needs to take out a new 30-year mortgage on their house. If the husband could not make the mortgage payment without the wife's income, they would have a permanent need for life insurance on the wife. Most permanent life insurance requires annual premium payments until age 100 or until death, whichever comes first. If the insured person is still alive at 100, usually no more premiums are required, but the life insurance stays in effect (wouldn't it be nice to get something for reaching age 100 besides odd questions about what you ate, what you drank, and whether you smoked filtered or unfiltered cigarettes?).

The Term Versus Permanent Decision

Criteria	Term	Permanent
How Long Do You Pay Premiums?	As long as you have coverage, which is usually a set number of years.	Coverage is usually for the lifetime of the insured individual, so are premiums.
Can the Annual Premium Change?	Yes and no. Yes, the cost of insurance goes up every year because older age means higher cost of insurance for the same amount of coverage. No, if you choose a 10-year or 20-year level term policy, the annual cost is fixed for that period of time.	With a basic whole life policy, the answer is no. The premium is fixed for life. With some of the new-fangled policies, the premium can increase.
Advantages	Annual premium does not change for a guaranteed time period. Cash outlay can be minimized for large amount of life insurance.	Premiums can be guaranteed for life. Some policies build a cash-in value. Some let you take a break from paying premiums or change the life insurance amount. Some let the owner direct how the policy's money is invested.
Disadvantages	Premiums increase dramatically after the initial guaranteed period. There is no cash build up in the policy.	The annual cash outlay is more than term. Greater cash is needed to fund the policy. If not set up correctly, some policies can *blow up* or require a surprise premium (more cash).

Secret #17: Long-term Care Insurance

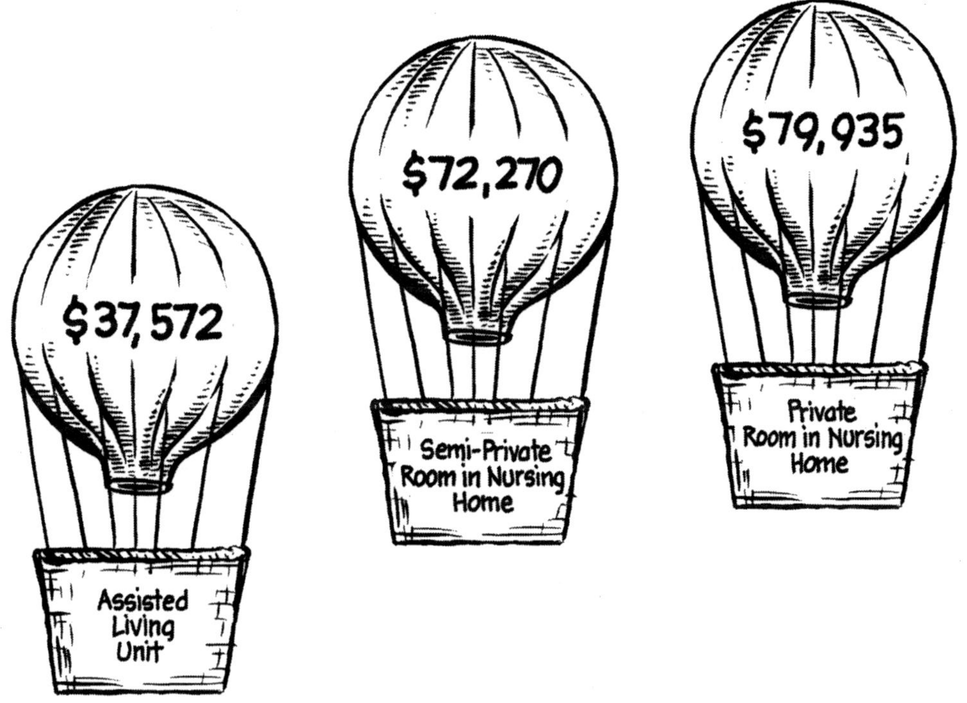

Long-term care is expennnnsssssive! The national average is $37,000 to $80,000 a year. For most people, figuring out the best way to pay for it is one of the final pieces in the retirement puzzle. With our aging population and life-extending medical advances, these costs are likely to rise each year. In 2010, there were about 9 million Americans over 65 who needed long-term care. By 2020, this number is expected to swell to 12 million!

What does it mean to need long-term care? Most medical and insurance definitions focus on a person's inability to do daily, routine activities unassisted – they are called the *Activities of Daily Living.* They include bathing, dressing, toileting, eating, and transferring (moving from a bed, a chair, or a vehicle with help). While it is impossible to predict which individuals will need long-term care, chances are that most people will require some form of long-term care during their lifetime.

My source: the U.S. Department of Health and Human Services' National Clearing House on Long-term Care Information website: longtermcare.gov on February, 1, 2011 (HHS Clearing House).

Seven Out of Every Ten Seniors Will Need Long-term Care

According to the HHS Clearing House, 70% of people age 65 or older will need some long-term care either on a temporary or permanent basis. On average, someone 65 years old will need long-term care for three years. Women typically need long-term care longer than men: 3.7 years for women versus 2.2 years for men. The next important question is:

What Could Long-term Care Cost You and Your Family?

If we multiply the average length of stay by the average annual cost of the different facilities, we can get a good idea of the total cost. For a lot of people, this is a real *eye-opener*!

How Will *You* Pay for Long-term Care?

Given the chance that you might need long-term care and the expense of that, the crucial question is, "How would you pay for it?" Think about that for a minute. In this section, I'm going to give you an overview of some of the common ways people deal with long-term care costs, which include Medicare, Medicaid, self-insurance, and private insurance (long-term care insurance). Some of the ways people attempt to deal with the costs of long-term care involve legal techniques. Please note that I am not an attorney, so you will find my comments about such techniques to be general in nature, especially as they relate to the topic of Medicaid.

Medicare: According to the HHS Clearing House, many consumers mistakenly believe that Medicare will pay for the long-term care services they might need. The reality is a different story. Medicare will only pay for long-term care if you need skilled nursing services or recuperative care for a short-period of time. Medicare will pay for up to 100 days of care, but only if two conditions are met: first, the long-term care must immediately follow a three-day minimum hospital stay, and second, you need skilled nursing services or the care is recuperative in nature. Medicare won't pay for what long-term care is mostly about: custodial care and help with activities of daily living. The bottom line is that Medicare is a short-term fix for what is likely to be a long-term need. 100 days is a *drop-in-the-bucket* when you consider that the average stay for long-term care is over 1,000 days. In other words, don't count on Medicare.

Medicaid: Medicaid is a joint federal and state program that provides a "safety net" for the poor. Among other forms of financial support, if you are truly broke, Medicaid will pay for your long-term care costs. While you won't have your choice of facilities or much privacy, Medicaid will pay for your stay in an assisted living facility or a nursing home.

Each state administers Medicaid and has its own rules about qualification. In general, you've got to spend your own money first. Depending on the state you live in, you are allowed to keep about $2,000 cash and certain assets like your home, one car, and a few other assets. If you are married, your spouse can retain certain assets and about $100,000 in cash. There are also income limits; if you have too much income, you won't qualify.

~~Federal and State Governments~~ Taxpayers Foot the Bill for Medicaid

According to the Cato Institute's website, downsizinggovernment.org, American taxpayers forked over 275 billion dollars for Medicaid in 2010. 92 billion of those dollars went to paying for long-term care. With an aging population and our current government's spending habits, expenditures for long-term care are likely to go up.

In order for Medicaid to remain a safety net for the poor, taxpayers cannot be expected to pay long-term care for people who can actually pay for it themselves. Taxpayer-funded Medicaid was never intended to pay for everyone's long-term care needs, especially those who can pay for it themselves (either out-of-pocket or by buying long-term care insurance). Unfortunately, there are some who believe that **you and I** should pay for their care so they can give their money to their family. Medicaid is for people who are really poor, not for those who are *pretending to be poor*.

In 2000, my grandmother began to suffer from declining health and dementia. With my family's assistance, she arranged to have health aides come into her home to help her with those activities of daily living. As her health declined further, one aide for an eight-hour daily shift became three aides for three shifts each day. It wasn't cheap. Wisely and fortunately, my grandmother had put aside some CDs (the same ones she taught me about back in 1980) to pay for this care. She proudly wrote checks to her aides until she physically couldn't do it anymore. My dad then wrote them out for her. My grandmother had the money (not a lot, but enough) to pay for her own care. She didn't try to hide the money or give it to her two sons in a dishonest attempt to qualify for Medicaid. If she had run out of money, then our family would have sought Medicaid. Honest Americans should do what my grandmother did; spend their own money first.

There are legitimate reasons to consult with an attorney about Medicaid, like planning and providing for the non-institutionalized spouse. Scheming to hide or give money to your family so you will *look* poor should not be one of the reasons. Join me on the next couple of pages to look at some legitimate ways to handle long-term care.

Your Table Is Ready, Sir.

Time for another table; I know you love them! They help us quickly compare different options. Here are some definitions, advantages, and disadvantages of the common ways people self-insure for long-term care:

Options if You Self-Insure

Option	**Definition**	**Advantage**	**Disadvantage**
Don't Do Anything	Literally, don't do anything about the risk of needing long-term care.	There's a 30% chance you won't need it, so no money or time is wasted.	You and your family will be unprepared for the costs and stress of getting you care.
Plan for Help at Home	Arrange for a health aide to come into the home. Modify your home as needed.	You stay in your own home! You are in control. You maintain your independence.	Around-the-clock care is costly. Less than 24-hour supervision could be risky.
Move in with the Kids	Pay to modify their home or help them buy a larger home.	They don't call it a *Mother-In-Law Suite* for nothing. Free care is a bargain!	Do you really want your kids to bathe you?
Buy into a Continuing Care Retirement Community (CCRC)	You pay an entrance fee plus monthly fees, kind of like a country club for long-term care.	They are set up to handle the different levels of care you might need as your health declines.	There is a wide range of choices, which could be confusing, and you've still got to come up with the cash to pay.

This is just an overview. You'll need to thoroughly investigate the specific options that best fit your individual needs. Keep in mind that some of the options can be combined together. (Mom, of course you can live with us, but I'm hiring a home health care aide to come in and help you with your daily bath.)

Think Ahead. Get Long-term Care Insurance.

The best time to look into long-term care insurance is yesterday. When the hurricane or tornado is bearing down on your house, the insurance company isn't going to sell you a wind damage policy! Please don't wait until you need care to try to buy long-term care insurance. You've got to get it while you are healthy. You don't know how healthy you will be a year from now, but you do know how healthy you are today. An insurance company will not issue you a long-term care policy if your health is declining. I usually tell anyone over 50 to consider long-term care insurance. Why? Long-term care isn't just for seniors. 40% of those currently receiving long-term care are adults between 18 and 64 years old (according to the HHS Clearing House). Also, the premiums for long-term care policies go up every year with age. You can lock-in a much lower premium at 60 years of age than if you wait until you are 70.

Policy Features	Advantage	Disadvantage
Premiums	$3,000 a year is a lot cheaper than $300,000 out-of-pocket for a nursing home stay.	Some require annual premium payments for the rest of your life. Premiums can go up.
Benefits	You can get coverage that provides care for the rest of your life.	Policy benefits and costs vary considerably and can be confusing. Get help from an agent.

The first and most important thing is that you need to find an experienced, **independent insurance agent** who can help you evaluate the choices. Some policies are very expensive, and some are suspiciously cheap. Some cover only certain types of care, while others cover just about everything. Some will actually let you cancel and get all your premiums back. Some have a death benefit for your family if you never use the policy. Lastly, some even allow you to make a *once-and-done* premium payment. A good long-term care insurance policy can reduce the potentially catastrophic impact that an extended stay in a facility would have on your finances and on your family. That's great peace-of-mind. So is the knowledge that you can pay for your care yourself. That would make my grandmother proud!

Secret #18: Annuities as Part of Your Retirement Plan

Before we take a look at *where* an annuity might fit into someone's retirement plan, let's first review the different types and basic features. An annuity is a legal contract between an insurance company and an individual. The contract isn't negotiable; the insurance company makes certain benefits and features available in the contract, and the consumer either accepts or rejects those terms. However, consumers have, quite literally, hundreds of annuities to choose from in the marketplace.

Ford Model T to *Lamborghini Gallardo* in 100 Years

Henry Ford introduced his Model T to the world in 1908. It had a 20 horsepower engine (www.ford.media.com accessed March 24, 2011). 100 years later, the Lamborghini Gallardo has an engine with 562 *horses* (accessed from Edmunds.com on March 24, 2011).

Over the years, annuity products have experienced the same robust growth and innovation as automobiles. Yet despite the wide variety available, all annuities can be assigned to two basic categories and three sub-categories:

Immediate Annuities	Deferred Annuities
• Single Life Income • Joint Life Income • Period Certain	• Traditional Fixed Annuity • Fixed Index Annuity • Variable Annuity

216 Billion Reasons Why Annuities Are Popular

A common misunderstanding about annuities is that there is just one type or that they are just one investment. As with mutual funds, there are many types. If you know or hear of someone who has a good or bad experience with an annuity, that really has nothing to do with what may be best for your individual situation. Stay focused on your specific needs.

The most basic definition of an annuity is that it is a series of equal payments guaranteed for a fixed period of time or for a person's lifetime. This is what is called an immediate annuity. The second type of annuity is called a deferred annuity. The deferred annuity allows the annuity owner to establish the annuity now and "defer" income until some future date.

According to *National Underwriter* "Are Annuity Sales Turning a Corner?" September 13, 2010, the majority of annuities purchased by individual consumers are deferred annuities. In the first half of 2010, about $108 billion went into annuities. $4 billion went into immediate annuities while $104 billion went into deferred annuities. Here's what those numbers look like for a whole year:

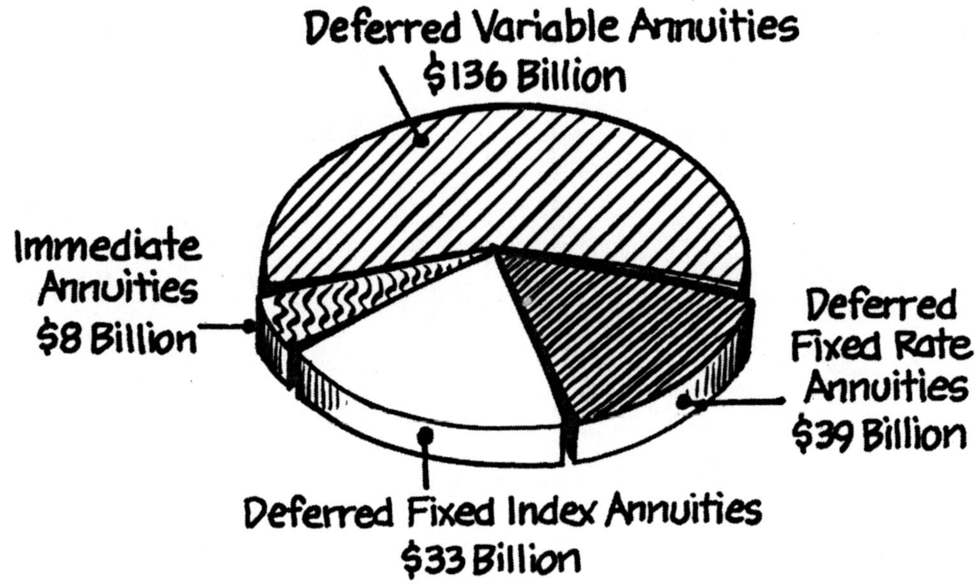

Immediate Annuities are the Opposite of Life Insurance

Insurance companies first introduced immediate annuities as a way for consumers to insure against the risk of dying *too late* (just the opposite of life insurance, which insures against the risk of dying *too soon*). For the lump sum paid to the insurance company, the buyer gets a steady stream of monthly income for the rest of his life. Since immediate annuities are irrevocable, a buyer should get a written quote of his monthly payments, before signing the paperwork. Payments depend on:

- Amount of the lump-sum (premium) paid
- Whether they are for a single life or joint life
- Owners' age and gender
- Life expectancy used by the insurance company
- Period certain or refund option (provides a guarantee of money to the owner's beneficiaries should the owner die pre-maturely)

Here's an example: A single woman in her mid-70s wants $1,000 per month for the rest of her life. She has no beneficiaries and is unconcerned about leaving her assets to anyone. To get her desired level of monthly income, she can make a lump-sum payment to an insurance company for about $150,000.

Ask an independent agent to be your personal shopper and find you the best income payout from a well-rated company. Why? For the same lump-sum payment, the guaranteed monthly income can vary between insurance companies. Income payments are based on the claims-paying ability of the issuing insurance company, so insurance company financial strength is an important consideration when purchasing any annuity.

Immediate annuities are often called "do-it-yourself-pensions" because you can create your own lifetime income. Ironically, this is exactly how many large businesses arrange for monthly pension payments to their retirees. The business writes a check to the insurance company, which then makes lifetime "pension" payments to the retirees.

Insurance companies are good at understanding that consumers want choices and flexibility. Because of this, immediate annuities were followed by an additional category of annuities called "deferred" annuities.

The Three Types of Deferred Annuities

Deferred annuity owners have the flexibility of making multiple, ongoing payments into their annuities, as well as the choice of when they want to start drawing income. This deferral allows the account to accumulate for a period of time before income payments begin. Often, there is still money left in deferred annuities when their owners die. The remaining value goes directly to the listed beneficiaries on the annuity contract. Here are some of the distinguishing features and limitations of deferred annuities:

Type	Key Features	Limitations
Traditional Fixed Annuity: also called Fixed Interest Annuity, Multi-Year Guaranteed Rate Annuity, or a Declared Rate Annuity	Principal is protected. Interest paid by the insurance company can be a fixed rate for the term of the annuity or be declared quarterly.	Interest paid can be better or worse than CDs for the same time commitment.
Fixed Index Annuity: also commonly called an Index Annuity	Principal is protected. Interest is credited by getting part of the increase in one or more stock market indices, which can produce attractive results. Fixed rate options are also usually available within the same annuity.	As a trade-off for principal protection granted, index-linked interest earnings can be zero when stock market results are poor. Interest earnings will not be as high as direct investments in the stock market.
Variable Annuity	Gains and losses are based on the direct investment in one or more sub-accounts within the annuity.	Principal is at risk just like other securities. There are a limited number of investments inside the annuity as opposed to a brokerage account, which can hold almost anything.

Common Characteristics of Deferred Annuities

Most deferred annuities share the following common characteristics:

- Surrender charges apply if the owner takes out more than 10% of the annuity's value each year during the annuity's contract term (also referred to as the "surrender period"). Surrender charges usually do not apply at death. Also, insurance companies will often waive or reduce surrender charges if the owner needs the money to pay for long-term care.

- At the death of the annuity's owner, the insurance company pays each designated beneficiary his or her share of what's left in the annuity (which is also not usually subject to probate).

- The accumulated value of the annuity can be "annuitized" to provide a lifetime income to the owner (like an immediate annuity).

- Due to the role they play in the lives of American investors and retirees, annuities are heavily regulated.

  - Variable annuities are considered securities, so they, and the brokers who sell them, are subject to federal oversight (SEC and FINRA) and state supervision.

  - Traditional fixed annuities, fixed index annuities, and immediate annuities are not securities, so they are only subject to state insurance department supervision.

- Although fixed annuities are guaranteed by the issuing company, each state has an insurance guaranty association which protects annuity owners in the event that an insurance company becomes insolvent. Once the company is found to be insolvent and a court ordered liquidation occurs, the guaranty association assumes responsibility for policy obligations and pays policy claims up to a specified dollar amount. The amount varies by state. Contact your state's guaranty association for limits and details.

Taxation of Annuities

Annuities receive favorable treatment under the current tax code. Deferred annuities "shelter" gains and interest earned from federal income taxes until withdrawals are taken. Immediate annuities also have their own special tax treatment. Here's an overview of how it works:

Annuity Type	Regular Money (Nonqualified)	IRAs and 401ks (Qualified)	Roth IRA
Immediate Annuity	Payments are only partially taxable as ordinary income because a portion of each payment you receive is your own money. This is called an *exclusion ratio.*	Every dollar that is withdrawn is taxed as ordinary income. Period.	Every dollar that is withdrawn is not subject to income taxes as long as you've had the Roth IRA for at least five years and you are at least 59½ years old.
Deferred Annuity	Accumulated interest comes out first and is taxed as ordinary income. Withdrawals of what you put in aren't taxed.*	Every dollar that is withdrawn is taxed as ordinary income. Period.	Every dollar that is withdrawn is not subject to income taxes as long as you've had the Roth IRA for at least five years and you are at least 59½ years old.

* Most deferred annuities allow the owner to "annuitize" their deferred annuity policy. This basically turns the deferred annuity into an immediate annuity. The tax treatment is much like an immediate annuity in that the "exclusion ratio" is then used to determine how much of each payment is taxable. Few people exercise this option because it is irrevocable, less flexible, and usually means nothing is left to the owner's beneficiaries.

Frequently Asked Questions about Annuities

How Long Do Annuity Surrender Charges Last?

Immediate annuities usually cannot be surrendered at all. The commitment period for the majority of deferred annuities is five to ten years. Mutual funds sold by brokers and bank-offered CDs both have surrender charges as well. A bond purchased prior to an interest rate jump has a "built-in surrender charge" because its value will go down 10% for every 1% increase in interest rates. That means that a 10-year bond purchased before rates go up 2% would be socked with a 20% reduction in its market value until either interest rates go back down or until the bond matures. You can't sell the bond early without losing 20%. Doesn't that sound just like a surrender charge? (Of course, the opposite can occur with both bonds and annuities when interest rates decline substantially; you can receive a gain for selling the bond or surrendering the annuity).

What if I Don't Want to Tie Up My Money? What Else Can I Do?

Presuming you want safety, here are your choices for principal protection: traditional fixed annuity, fixed index annuity, money market, CDs, and bonds (but only if you hold them to maturity). If you are unable to commit your funds for a period of time, then you are only left with the money market, bonds, and short-term CDs. You can't have it both ways. Money market accounts don't pay 7%. If you want decent guaranteed returns and/or the potential to earn even higher returns, then you've got to give the investment or insurance company a commitment. They need to know that they can work with your money for a while and invest it longer term.

If you don't care about safety, then buy securities from a broker or hire a fee-based investment adviser to pick mutual funds and securities for you.

Is Putting an IRA into an Annuity a Waste of a Tax-Shelter?

According to the *National Underwriter* article I cited earlier, about $100 billion of IRA money went into annuities in 2010. More often than not, the primary reason annuities are recommended is for their principal protection and the lifetime income guarantees. Tax deferral is a nice feature for nonqualified money, but is irrelevant for IRAs.

Frequently Asked Questions about Annuities

How Are Advisers Paid for Selling Annuities?

Insurance agents get a 3 to 7% commission on most annuities. Likewise, brokers typically get 4 to 5% for selling "A" and "B" share mutual funds (the exact percentage depends on the amount of the sale). For some perspective, keep in mind that realtors get 5 to 7% for selling a house.

How Do I Know My Adviser Is Recommending the Best Annuity?

Ask if he is an employee of an insurance company, and ask how many insurance companies he can use. Ask him to walk you through his selection process.

Aren't Annuities Complicated?

Cars are complicated, but you still drive one. Some financial products are more complex than others, but if you are working with a competent adviser, complexity won't be an issue, because he or she will explain the annuity's features, benefits, costs, and limitations to you in plain English.

What if My Broker Says That Annuities Are Bad?

If someone tells you all annuities are bad, they will usually make sweeping generalizations about performance, costs, and surrender charges. Most annuities are not designed to compete directly with stocks. By the way, annuities are the *only* financial product or investment that can provide a guarantee of lifetime income. Those who recommend competing products always seem to omit this fact when they are beating annuities up and talking them down.

If a broker recommends against a particular type of annuity, you need to ask him two simple, yet revealing questions: 1. Is he licensed to sell the particular annuity he is bashing? 2. Does his employer have an agreement with the insurance company that allows him to sell it? If he can't sell it for either reason, then you'll need to go somewhere else to get it. The broker certainly won't want that! Read the next section, "The Financial Services War," for an expanded explanation.

The Financial Services War

There is a full-scale war raging right now on American soil! The war, which usually goes unnoticed by the general public, is between the securities industry and the insurance industry. So, what's it all about? It is a battle over where people will invest their money.

According to the Investment Company Institute's website (www.ici.org) accessed on February 1, 2011, roughly 339 billion dollars flowed into mutual funds and ETFs during 2010. If you recall the statistic I gave you earlier in this chapter, roughly 216 billion went into annuities during the same period. While money moves around all the time between stocks, bonds, money market accounts, and other investments, it is easy to see what the *fighting is all about* – simply look at the combined total of what went into mutual funds, ETFs and annuities during 2010:

Because I utilize both securities and insurance products to build financial plans for my clients, I have watched this "War" since 1992. My opinion is that the securities industry has recently stepped up their attacks on insurance products because they fear losing their share of the money. The securities industry and their accomplices in the media have been working overtime trying to convince investors that "annuity" is a four-letter-word. Why? It's a tug-of-war; if *more* money flows into insurance products and annuities, *less* goes into mutual funds and other securities.

Flagrant Media Bias and the Baby Boomer Gold Rush

It used to be that we could trust magazines and newspapers to adhere to journalistic principles, but not anymore. Today, some journalists start with the desired conclusions and then conduct interviews and research that will support those conclusions, or they simply ignore the facts completely. If you see a magazine or newspaper article that skewers a particular financial product or investment, first take a look at their advertisers. For example, you will probably never see a positive article about annuities in *Money Magazine*. Why? Perhaps because there are over a dozen paid advertisements in *Money Magazine* for brokers and investments that compete directly with annuities.

The securities industry and the insurance industry have been competitors for a long time. So what has changed to ratchet up the fight?

1. Four "down" years for the stock market during the first decade of the new millennium, that's what. Many rattled investors sought the downside protection and income guarantees offered by annuities.

2. The baby boomers are coming. There are 76 million Americans who were born between 1946 and 1964. 10,000 baby boomers will retire each day until the end of 2029. Both industries are well aware that baby boomers need help planning their retirements (and the fact that baby boomers stand to inherit <u>trillions of dollars</u> from their parents isn't lost on anyone either). So both industries are pushing and shoving for their place by the river, so they can *pan for their share of baby boomer gold.* Naturally, the securities industry wants baby boomers to keep all their money invested in the market. The insurance industry thinks that annuities and insurance products can help make baby boomers' retirements more secure.

As a CERTIFIED FINANCIAL PLANNER™ practitioner, who is licensed to provide both annuities and investment advice, I can tell you that <u>both</u> sides in the "War" are right. Annuities can be a good choice for a guarantee of lifetime income and protection of principal, while mutual funds and other securities can offer the opportunity for inflation-fighting growth. Often, I find that a solid financial plan will need a mix of both in order to meet an individual client's objectives.

Conclusion

You are retired or want to be someday. You know the outcome you need and you know the threats. What's next? All kinds of would-be-experts are going to tell you what you should do with your money. The financial services business can out spin politics any day of the week! You can expect bias. An insurance company salesperson will promote his or her company as the best one on the whole planet.

Today's consumers are bombarded by a steady stream of:

- *Sensationalized* TV programming
- *Alarmist* radio shows
- *Biased* newspaper reporting
- *Advertiser-friendly* magazine articles
- *Unsolicited* email
- *Product-pitching* financial seminars

To find information you can trust, you have to pay attention, ask questions, and look for objectivity. Use common sense. Listen to your gut. If the pitch sounds too good to be true…run.

Keeping this in mind, "people" and "products" *are* the tools you will use to build a secure retirement. You may hire people to build a personalized plan and to buy investment and financial products. When you do find the *right* adviser to help you put together a retirement plan to meet your needs, hold onto him or her. Great advice can be the difference between a secure retirement and one that is hugely disappointing.

Never forget that it is *your* money and *your* retirement. Sometimes, to make your retirement work, you will need to change advisers and swap out your financial tools for better ones. You must always do what is best for you, your family and your situation. No one cares more about your retirement than you do.

A Few Final Words from My Compliance Department

David D. Holland is an Investment Adviser Representative of Holland Advisory Services, Inc. Investment advisory services are offered through Holland Advisory Services, Inc., a registered investment advisory firm. Insurance and annuity products are offered through Holland Insurance Services, Inc. Holland Advisory Services and Holland Insurance Services are separate affiliated companies and share common ownership under Holland Financial, Inc.

David D. Holland is a licensed Certified Public Accountant with the State of Florida Board of Accountancy and is a CERTIFIED FINANCIAL PLANNER™ practitioner in good standing with the Certified Financial Planner Board of Standards.

Certified Financial Planner Board of Standards, Inc. owns the certification marks CFP®, CERTIFIED FINANCIAL PLANNER™ and federally registered CFP (with flame design) in the U.S., which it awards to individuals who successfully complete CFP Board's initial and ongoing certification requirements.

CPSIA information can be obtained at www.ICGtesting.com
227867LV00002BA/1/P

LU000588575 27